Conflict Resolution through Negotiation, Mediation, Arbitration, and Litigation

DORIS YVONNE MARSHALL PhD

OB

ISBN:
978-1-952874-98-7 (paperback)
978-1-952874-97-0 (ebook)

Published by:

⦿ OMNIBOOK Co.

OMNIBOOK CO.
99 Wall Street, Suite 118
New York, NY 10005
USA
+1-866-216-9965
www.omnibook.org

First Edition

For e-book purchase: Kindle on Amazon, Barnes and Noble
Book purchase: Amazon.com, Barnes & Noble, and
www.omnibook.org

Omnibook titles may be purchased in bulk for educational,
business, fund-raising, or sales promotional use. For more
information please e-mail admin@omnibook.org

ACKNOWLEDGMENTS

I would like to express my appreciation to my husband, Byford Dan Marshall, for his loving support and encouragement throughout my educational experience. I would also like to express my appreciation to my children for their support, patience and understanding of the times I could not be with them due to my studies.

A special appreciation goes to Robbie Thompson for all her kindness and support toward me. I would never have been able to accomplish my goal without the loving and caring people in my life.

TABLE OF CONTENTS

Chapter Four
New Approaches to Resolving Conflict

Chapter Five
Gaining a Satisfactory Resolution: Substantive Satisfaction, Procedural Satisfaction and Psychological Satisfaction

Chapter Six
God Tailors the Events of Our Lives

chapter one

ABSTRACT

The available findings support that conflict is defined as a dispute, difference or disagreement between two or more rational persons over something one person wants from someone else, which that person refused to grant. It is important to note that conflict is not necessarily undesirable or negative; but instead, the tensions prevalent in conflict can often be a collaborative for creative solutions to problems.

Most of us are constantly negotiating with each other. Negotiation is, and has been the first and foremost way in which to prevent and resolve disputes. Agreement is the way in which free people seek to resolve their differences. The process is bilateral with parties themselves making the final decision to agree or disagree.

Mediation is an adjunct to negotiation. In mediation, a third party, or a mediator, enters the process to help the disputants agree with each other. The parties in dispute remain the final decision makers and they remain in pursuit of getting what they want by agreement.

Arbitration is decision making by a third party. Arbitration, as well as mediation, is voluntary. A good arbitrator is focused on the merits of the opposing claims.

Litigation is third party decision making by the courts or an administrative agency. Unlike mediation and arbitration, which can only be involved by agreement, litigation can be commenced by either side. The judicial system, or applicable statute, determines whether a judge, panel of judges, or jury should be the final decision maker.

We are experiencing so much conflict in our society the need for more mediation is great. In this study, an effort was made to agree to negotiate, gather points of view, focus or interests, create win-win options and to create an agreement.

chapter two

REVIEW OF
RELATED MATERIAL

NEGOTIATION

During the Colonial Period in the United States, courts and lawyers were not the people's preferred choice for dispute resolution. Colonists preferred a community type settlement because they distrusted lawyers or the court system to uphold their interests. During the seventeenth century, many civil disputes, and even criminal disputes were heard by local church tribunals. Therefore, the community way of settling disputes encompassed community values with an ideology based upon religion or ethics and the geographic or commercial interests of the local community in mind.[1] Disputes were settled face to face. Community mediation in the United States is as old as the pilgrims. All disputes were settled within the community to foster unity and strength. If the individual did not comply with the community sanction, they were physically cast out and isolated. The community maintained order and peace among its citizens via shared community values. As shared community values gave way to individual rights in the civil law arena.

During the Industrial Revolution in the United States, the concept of community values declined. New wealth and power birthed a new social order.

---

1   Peter L. Berger and Richard J. Neuhaus, 1977, "To Empower People: The Role of Mediation Structure in Public Policy," Washington D.C.: American Enterprise Institute for Public Policy Research.

The early years of the twentieth century were a period of mass immigration to the United States. True community dispute resolution was reborn because it served a purpose in the immigrant communities.[2] However, as new immigrants began to integrate into the American culture, they began to adopt the independent, twentieth century American social values of industrialization, urbanism and professionalism. The assimilation of immigrants was aided by a legal system that upheld individual rights. The concept of individual rights increased, so did the struggle between community and the courts as a means of absorbing social conflict and maintaining social control.

During the early nineteen hundreds, it became apparent that the existing court system was in a state of crisis. An overburdened, costly and ineffective court system meant delayed justice, and justice only for the rich. As a result of this crisis, Justice Roscoe Pound sounded the alarm for court reform in order to aid social stability and justice.[3] As a result of reforms in the legal systems, there was an expansion of courts, social service agencies, and lawyers. Government reform greatly expanded the court system as a means of solving social conflict and social problems. However, as the legal system grew in complexity, Justice Pound remarked that there were intrinsic limitations upon effective legal action. In other words, Justice Pound meant that not every social problem has a legal solution.

Due to the complexity of the court system and increased government intervention via the courts, American capitalists increased their use of arbitration as a means of circumventing the overburdened court system. As a fearful response, lawyers brought arbitration within the legal system, and by 1950, three-fourths of all commercial litigation was diverted to arbitration.[4]

In the 1960s, the social movement rekindled the idea of community and popular justice. Additionally, the idea emerged that

---

2   Jay Folberg, 1983, "A Mediation Overview: History and Dimensions of Practice.", Mediation Quarterly. San Francisco: Jossey Bass.
3   Christine B. Harrington, 1985, Shadow Justice: The Ideology and Institutionalization of Alternatives to Court, Boston: Little, Brown, and Company, 139- 162.
4   Craig A. McEwen, and Richard J. Mainman, 1982, "Arbitration and Mediation as Alternatives to Court," Policies Studies Journal, 10: 712-725.

disputes were a form of property that belonged to the community.[5] The riots of 1968 also prompted using mediation as a form for settling racial disputes. In fact, the Community Relations Service was established earlier under the Civil Rights Act of 1964 to utilize mediation and conciliation to resolve community racial conflict.[6] Additionally, it was even discussed that criminal disputes could be handled by a form of African tribal moat.[7] Interwoven within all of these concepts was the fundamental idea of the community absorbing conflict in such a manner that individual values were excluded.

In 1976, the American Bar Association, amid the scandals of Watergate and fearing public dissatisfaction with the legal system, declared the courts of Alternative Dispute Resolution (ADR), because it was an inexpensive and speedy form of justice. Conceptually, ADR was taken from the realm of community empowerment and reformed into a procedural solution to an ailing legal system. Practically, ADR was employed by the legal systems as a means of self preservation. Formally, alternative dispute resolution was proposed as a way for underprivileged citizens to resolve their problems quickly and at minimal expense. Officially, neighborhood justice centers were established throughout the country because Chief Justice Warren Burger had suggested that neighbor tribunals should be established to handle minor claims.[8] Therefore, the concept of community finally became legitimized, although not in its original colonial form. Although historically, alternative forms of dispute resolution have been on the private or public septemic policy agenda since colonial times, the institutionalization of ADR as public policy in the United States did not officially take place until the passage of the Dispute Resolution Act in 1980. The evolution of this federal public policy will be discussed in the following sections.

Politically, the key agenda issue, access to justice for the poor and powerless, was a battle over the delivery and distribution of legal

---

5   Wright, 1989.
6   James Laue, 1989, "The Conflict Resolution Movement: History, Problems, and Prospects" in Christian, T.F. (Ed.) Expanding Horizons: Theory and Research in Dispute
7   Folberg, 1983.
8   Bureau of national Affairs, Inc., 1985 and Harrington, 1985.

resources. Politically defined, legal resources were considered the institutions that fostered negotiation and mediation.

Therefore, the political agenda issue was one of an institutional nature, not one of a legal nature, although an individual's right of access to justice was directly affected.

During the late 1970s, community groups led nationally by consumer advocate Ralph Nader, pushed for a national consumer program and opposed both the Justice Department's and the American Bar Association's involvement in the Commerce Committee's proposed federal programs. The Nader groups were against expanding legal advocacy. In the meanwhile, the Senate and House Judiciary Committees were working on an informal mechanism to handle a range of minor criminal and civil disputes, not only consumer problems.[9] Nader's community groups challenged this legalistic approach on the basis that if both criminal and civil disputes were merged into one process, any resemblance of consumer protection would be effectively destroyed.

During the legislative debates, the focus was upon the difference between resolving disputes, unresolved conflict and representing the unrepresented disputes. In the final analysis, the more conservative consumer groups joined with the conservative elites to form a coalition of such strength that the Nader activists could not win the battle.

The State of Texas was among the first to enact ADR enabling legislation. In 1983, the Texas legislature passed an act authorizing the Commissioner's Court of each county to establish an alternative dispute resolution system, similar to the federal act, and to collect money for the system by levying a tax on court case filing fees.

In measuring the criteria of games theory, negotiation and mediation are games of strategy, while arbitration and litigation are predominantly games of skill. However, negotiation also can require skill and players in arbitration and litigation are required to make strategic decisions. Chance can also be a factor in most games. The dominant influence in negotiation, with or without mediation, is the

---

9   Christine B. Harrington, Shadow Justice: The Ideology and Institutionalization of Alternatives to Court, Westport: Greenwood Press, 1985.

interaction of the parties based on their expectations of each other's behavior.

Mediation is also a game of strategy, since the moves of the mediator depend on the actions and reactions of the negotiators. However, the mediator has a different incentive than negotiators whose goal is the best deal they can get for their side. The mediator's goal is to get both sides to agree with each other.

On many occasions, chance can influence the outcome. In arbitration and litigation, the disputants are called upon to convince the arbitrator, judge or jury to decide in their favor. This challenge can require skills, even though the disputants are sometimes called upon to make strategic decisions.

Negotiation Basics

The unabridged second edition of The Random House Dictionary defines negotiation as the mutual discussion of the terms of a transaction or agreement. The College Edition also defines negotiation as mutual discussion, but it correctly adds the words aiming at an agreement, at least for most negotiations. However, discussion is not indispensable. Negotiation can be tacit as well as explicit. Example: Automobile drivers tacitly agree with each other on who goes first,

Agreement requires mutual consent, and negotiation includes the possibility of a disagreement. Therefore, parties may discuss terms of settlement; but, they can also refuse to agree to the terms demanded by the other side.

Negotiation means both sides have the right to disagree with each other, the right to say no, and to be meaningful about it. The right to say no must include the power to do something about it. Sometimes this is referred to as bargaining strength, or leverage.

The negotiator's bargaining strength is the product of his readiness to walk away from the bargaining table to the disadvantage of the other party. If the negotiator is able to convince the other side that he is prepared to walk, whether or not he means what he says. A negotiator's skill may include his ability to mislead his opponent about his true bargaining strength. That is why both parties may enter into a dispute with their mind closed to any changes in their position. Example: A demand for unconditional surrender leaves no room for negotiation. Therefore, the ideal situation in negotiation is what is sometimes referred to as a level playing field with each side possessing relatively equal bargaining strength. The right and power to say no are indispensable ingredients of a true negotiation, even though the extent of a negotiator's bargaining strength may vary with his power to say no. Example: A man/woman begging for food may plead for alms, but little can be done if turned down.

Negotiating from strength or weakness lies in the ability of the negotiator to say no and confidently end the discussion. The Constitution of the United States requires the advice and consent of the Senate before a Supreme Court Justice can be seated. The Senate can bargain in negotiating with the President, since it has the unqualified right and power to say no.

At the time of this writing, a marathon of non-stop negotiations were being conducted in an effort to end a nationwide crippling strike of the Teamsters Union and United Parcel Service. "The walkout of 185,000 Teamster members, who work as package sorters, loaders and delivery truck drivers at United Parcel Service, began on August 4 after failure to reach agreement on a new contract."[10] As yet they have failed to reach any agreement that could end the union's walk out against the nation's dominant package delivery service. The Teamsters proposal for more full time jobs, and the company's call for a new pension system limited to United Parcel Service workers. The sessions involved face-to-face discussions between United Parcel Service and Teamster representatives, and then separate caucuses for each side. Despite the round the clock discussions, both sides seemed prepared for a long strike. Although crippled, with their high volume of 12 million packages carried per day slowed to a trickle of about ten percent, the nation's dominant package delivery service company carried on business as usual.[11]

---

10   The Lufkin Daily News, Sunday, August 17, 1997, 6A.
11   Ibid.

Negotiation Additional Considerations

During the course of a negotiation, individuals representing themselves need consult with no one. They can be represented or advised by a lawyer. The lines of communications are relatively simple.

In group situations the lines of communication become more complicated. Corporations, unions and government agencies have no separate corporeal existence. They are inanimate entities created by individuals pursuant to laws passed by other individuals and their existence is simply a figment of the law. These groups can only act through individuals.

Individuals designated to represent group entities are selected by other individuals with authority to make decisions. They may act in concert, but their decision making is frequently dominated by a single individual. Groups have no independent capacity to act. They can only think and act through individuals. In any event, all such individuals are representatives of the groups. However they arrive at decisions, their collective wishes are usually carried out by a designated spokesmen who may be officials of the group or outsiders retained for that related purpose. You may have many individuals involved in the negotiation process; yet, there can only be one chief spokesman and ultimate decision maker.

As the eminent British philosopher Walter Bagelot once said, "When two men ride on a horse, one has to ride in front."[12] In negotiation there are two horses to ride, one of the individuals who is the chief spokesman for his side and the other for the individuals, or individuals who are the chief decision makers, he rarely comes to the bargaining table. The labor/management director acts as the chief spokesman. The top official union chief will be the spokesman for the labor organization. However, any agreement reached must almost invariably be submitted to the rank and file for ratification.

Conflict resolution representatives on the front line must first agree with their principals on goals, strategies, tactics, reassess and

---

12   Lowry, 243.

modify them as the conflict runs its course. In turn, the principal can be a single individual or a committee.

The individuals deciding on these matters negotiate with each other. In this effect, negotiation not only goes on between the disputants, but also between and among the principals on both sides.

There can be a great amount of differences between ongoing relationships in which the parties must continue to live with each other after the dispute is over and disputes are growing out of first and last time negotiations in which the disputants are unlikely ever to see each other again. However, in one shot dealings, the focus can be primarily on the present. In the ongoing relationship, the past and future inform and shape the present.

The party endeavoring a change in the status quo has the burden of going forward with proposals. If they are denied, the party in control remains in possession of the status quo. It is then up to the party wanting a change to decide whether to accept the status quo and abandon the negotiations or to take steps that shift the burden of responding to the other side.

The principle of the burden going forward is well illustrated by the practices of labor and management in the negotiation of collective bargaining agreements. In the past, labor/management negotiations most often began with a union's demand for a wage increase. If the employer turns down the increase, the union's traditional response was to strike. Today, with the high cost of strikes, unions will think twice before calling one.

On the other hand, if the employer proposes a wage decrease and the union refuses to accept the cut, the company can either abandon its demand or respond by unilaterally imposing the cut.

The media can also play a major role in the negotiation process. The lines of communication can become especially complex in situations involving groups with large constituencies, as governments, publicly held companies, unions, political organizations and special interest groups. In this situation, the media can and does play an important roll. Skilled negotiators often use the threat of the media to communicate with the opposite side, to convey threats, promises, bargaining strength and determination, to send signals or to float trial balloons. Disputants at times wish to avoid public attention and they may be sensitive to publicity and concerned about untimely or untoward disclosure that might impair their bargaining positions.

Little Red Riding Hood and Wolf Negotiate

Fairytales and folktales are read to children to entertain them, but these stories also communicate common ideas and modes of thinking about relationships, morals, values, and how to get along in the world. Fairytales present children with a model of how to think and act. In the original story of Little Red Riding Hood, one of the morals is to beware of strangers, one good, one bad, one innocent, one cunning, one right, one wrong. If the retelling of the story seemed odd, it is because it challenges the stereotype of the Big Bad Wolf and asks us to consider his side of the story.

The tenets of conflict resolution present a new model of interacting with and thinking about other people, one that challenges us to go beyond stereotypes, to consider the other's point of view, and to reach mutually satisfactory agreements in which all parties win. The story is an illustration of one of the problem solving processes of conflict resolution. If we can succeed in teaching our youth this framework for resolving their disputes, the results for them and for our society could be profound.

In step one, Little Red Riding Hood agrees to take turns talking and listening as well as cooperating to solve the problems. The bad wolf agrees to take turns talking, listening, and cooperating with Little Red Riding Hood to solve the problems, as well. As the story is told, both agree to negotiate.[13]

In step two, Red Riding Hood and the wolf gather points of view. Red presented her side of the story saying she was taking a loaf of fresh bread and some cakes to her granny's cottage on the other side of the woods. Granny had not been feeling well, so Red stopped to

---

13   R. Bodine, R.D. Crawford, and F. Schrumpt, 1994, Creating the Peaceable School: A
      Comprehensive Program for Teaching Conflict Resolution, Champaign, IL: Research
      Press, Inc., 112.

pick some flowers for her along the way. The wolf jumped out from behind a tree and started asking a lot of questions. All the time, the wolf was grinning a wicked grin, smacking his lips together, and being gross and rude. Wolf listened carefully, repeating her main ideas back to her, to be perfectly clear. Then Red Riding Hood listened to Wolf present his side, stating that the forest is his home. He cares about it and tries to keep it clean. He was busy cleaning up garbage people had left behind when he heard footsteps. He told Red he hid behind a tree and saw her coming down the trail looking suspicious dressed in that strange red cape with her head covered up as if she was hiding and did not want anyone to see her face. Then she began picking his flowers and stepping on his new little pine trees. When he asked her what she doing, she gave him a song and dance about going to her granny's house with a basket of goodies. Of course, that made Wolf unhappy about the way she treated him or his home. Red reiterated Wolfs concerns back to him for confirmation.[14]

Red Riding Hood responded that the problem didn't stop there because when she arrived at her granny's house, Wolf was disguised in her granny's nightgown and tried to eat her with his big ugly teeth. She feared she might have been killed if the woodsman had not come in and saved her. Red stated Wolf scared her granny so bad that she hid under the bed. Wolf carefully considered her statements and agreed that he had disguised himself in her granny's nightgown; but his masquerade had a purpose. He told Red that he happened to know her granny and after allowing her to go on her way, he had run ahead to granny's cottage to discuss with her what had happened. They agreed that Red needed a lesson, and that was when he disguised himself in her nightgown and granny hid under the bed. Then Red Riding Hood made a nasty remark about his ears, which he was sensitive about, but he tried to make the best of it by saying his big hears helped him to hear her better. Next, she hurt his feelings about his big eyes and he found it hard to tum the other cheek, but he managed by telling her his big eyes helped him to see her better.

---

14   Ibid.

Red's next insult about his big teeth really got to him because he was especially sensitive about his teeth. That was when he lost control and leaped from the bed and growling that his teeth would help him to eat her. Wolf felt that everyone knew no wolf could ever eat a girl, but she was screaming and running around the house so fast he could not catch her to calm her down. Wolf stated he knew he was in big trouble when the door suddenly came crashing open and"... a big woodsman stood there with his ax ... there was an open window behind me, so out I went."[15] Terrible rumors circulated through the forest about Wolf because Red Riding Hood had called him a Big Bad Wolf and he had been hiding ever since. He was unhappy and felt bad, afraid to show his face in the forest.

He did not understand why Granny had not told his side of the story and cleared up the situation. Wolf felt miserable and lonely and that he had been treated unfairly. Red Riding Hood's responded that granny had been very tired, ill, and confused lately and couldn't remember what had happened. They deduced that granny was sick and had just forgotten their agreement that Red needed to be taught a lesson. [16]

In step three, the two parties focus on their interests. Red begins by explaining that she wants to be able to take flowers to Granny to help cheer her up, and she wants to go through the forest to Granny's house because it is too far to take the road around the forest and it is a fun place. She also said she wanted the wolf to stop trying to scare her or threaten her in the forest because she wanted to feel safe. Wolf advised that he wanted to keep is forest home looking nice and he wanted her to watch where she walked and stop picking his flowers. He also wanted the rumors stopped; he wanted to be liked, and able to enjoy the forest without being hunted down. He felt the forest was his home and he should be free to enjoy it.[17]

In step four, Red and Wolf strive to create win-win options. Red thoughtfully began by stating she could try to stay on the path when walking through the forest, in order to solve the problem.

---

15   Ibid.
16   Ibid.
17   Ibid.

Wolf reasoned if she would do that, he could be more cooperative by remembering to call out when he heard her coming instead of quietly stepping out from behind a tree, and he could plant some flowers by Granny's house for her to pick. Red volunteered to pick up trash as she walked through the forest and put it in granny's trash can. Since granny was Wolf's friend too, he offered to check on her to make sure she was okay on the days Red could not come. Red said she could inform her friends that she was not afraid of Wolf anymore; he could be nice. Also, she and granny would speak to the woodsman and tell him they had made a mistake about him. Wolf then proposed he could meet her friends and show them through the forest.[18]

In step five, our characters evaluate their options. Wolf wanted reassurance that he would not have to worry about the woodsman or hunters after she informed the woodsman she had made a mistake about Wolf. He asked if he could go with her when she talked to the woodsman. Red agreed to that and offered to take him with her when she told her friends she was not afraid of him anymore. She volunteered to help him plant the flowers and was glad to have him visit her lonely granny too. Wolf said he did not think she should have to stay on the path all the time and offered to show her where to walk and not harm anything. This pleased Red, but she questioned whether he really thought he could check on granny when she could not visit. Wolf offered the solution to that issue by having Red call him early in the morning. Red came up with the idea of asking her friends for a donation when they went for a tour of the forest. She figured they could use the money to buy more trees to plant and even start a recycling program for the trash they picked up. They found solutions to benefit both of them.[19]

In step six, they laid out their plans. Red agreed that after talking to granny she would make an arrangement to go see the woodsman that afternoon and let Wolf know the appointed time. Wolf agreed he would draw up a possible forest tour map for her and get some flowers to plant at granny's by Saturday. Red pledged to bring some friends over to try out Wolfs tour map after he completed it, and introduce

18   Ibid.
19   Ibid.

them to him, showing them he was nice. Wolf promised he would put a donation box at the edge of the forest for their recycling program. Red mentioned again that she would call him by 7:00 a.m. if she was unable to go check on her granny. These settlements sounded great to both characters. "... (The two shake hands.)"[20]

Disputants in negotiation have sole responsibility for the outcome. Introduction of mediation does not end negotiation. Mediation is an adjunct to negotiation. In mediation the disputants remain the final decision makers. The subject matters of the controversy and the time frame also remains the same. The mediator is there simply to help the negotiators get together.

There are many conflicts that can be properly resolved only through confrontation, confession, forgiveness, and cooperative negotiation. But there are hundreds more that can be properly resolved simply by overlooking minor offenses, relinquishing rights for the sake of God's kingdom. Therefore, before focusing on your rights, take a careful look at your responsibilities; and before you go to remove the speck from your brother's eye, ask yourself, is this really worth fighting over?

Differentiate the material issues from the personal issues when you find yourself involved in conflict. Determine which personal issues are having the greatest influence on you and on your opponent. Question what the other person involved in the conflict has done that has offended you.

When you find yourself in conflict with anyone or anything, check your attitude to ascertain why or if you can rejoice in the Lord in this situation. Ask yourself whether you have been irritable, rude, or abrasive in this situation. From this point on, when or how can you make a special effort to be forbearing, large hearted, gentle, courteous, considerate, generous, lenient, or moderate. Search yourself and discover how could your gentleness be more evident to others. Determine what you have been worried or anxious about and remember how God has shown Himself to be loving, powerful, and faithful to you in previous conflicts or difficulties. Pinpoint what you

---

20   Ibid.

would like Him to do for you, or accomplish through this conflict. Honestly thing about what is good about the person with whom you are in conflict, what is right about his concerns, any good memories you may have of your relationship with him, and how has God helped you through that person. Uncover the principles taught in Scripture are most difficult for you to put into practice in this situation and decide whether you will apply those principles, and if so, how you will proceed to do so.

More important determinations to make are what effect this dispute is having or likely to have on your family life, your occupation, your finances or property, your friendships, your relationship with God, and your service to your church and community.

Consider what legal rights could you exercise in this situation. Would it be morally right to do so? How might exercising these rights glorify God, advance his kingdom, benefit others and benefit you? How might laying down these rights glorify God, advance His kingdom, benefit others, and benefit you?

After you have decided exactly what has offended you, evaluate and determine which of the offenses you could simply overlook, and how might doing so please and honor God. Then examine the material issues involved in the dispute and decide which of these you can simply give in on.[21]

Whenever you are involved in conflict, it is important to consider if you may be contributing to the problem, either directly or indirectly. In some cases, you may have caused the controversy. In others, you may have aggravated a dispute by failing to respond to another person in a godly way. Therefore, before focusing on what others have done wrong, it is wise to carefully examine the way you have been thinking, speaking, and acting.

Although it is often best simply to overlook the sins of others, there will be times when doing so only prolongs alienation and encourages them to continue acting in a hurtful manner. If you know that someone has something against you, go to that person and talk about it even before you worship God. Moreover, if another person's

---

21   Ibid., 77-78.

sins are dishonoring God, damaging your relationships, hurting others, or hurting that person, one of the most loving and helpful things you can do is to lovingly show that sinner where there is a need for change. With God's help and the right words including your own confession, such a conversation will often lead to restored peace and a stronger relationship.[22]

Ron Kraybill, a respected Christian mediator, has noted that effective confrontation is like a graceful dance from supportiveness to assertiveness and back again.[23] Negotiation does not have to be a painful tug of war. If approached properly, many people will respond favorably to cooperative negotiation, which can allow you to find mutually beneficial solutions to common problems. Sometimes, all it takes is a willingness to look not only to your own interests, but also to the interests of others.

The principles described in Romans 12:14-21 are applicable at every stage of conflict, and they are echoed throughout the Bible. Love your neighbor as yourself. Do to others what you would have them do to you. Overlook an offense. If someone is caught in a sin, restore him gently. Speak the truth in love. Look out for the interests of others. Forgive as the Lord forgave you. Do not be overcome by evil, but overcome evil with good. Applying these principles can be difficult, but it is always worth the effort, because God works in and through us as we serve Him as peacemakers. Paul promises: "Therefore, my dear brothers, stand firm. Let nothing move you, always give yourself fully to the work of the Lord, because you know that your labor in the Lord is not in vain" (1 Corinthians 15:58).[24]

We have learned negotiation is a personal bargaining process in which parties seek to reach a mutually agreeable settlement of their differences. Although some people are able to negotiate for themselves, many rely on attorneys or other professionals to advise them or act on their behalf.[25]

---

22   Ibid., 125-126.
23   Ibid., 143.
24   Ibid., 203.
25   Ibid., 213.

TEN COMMANDMENTS FOR NEGOTIATORS

1. In the words of eminent Scottish poet Robert Burns, try to see yourself as others see you.

2. Strive also to see others as they see themselves.

3. Clearly define the issues at the outset of the dispute.

4. Remember, you can't argue about a fact, but only be ignorant of it.

5. Bluffing and puffing in the manner of the buyer in the Bible's Proverbs, is permissible: "It is naught, saith the buyer; but when he is gone his way, then he boasteth."

6. False statements of facts are not permissible. As the Bible's Proverbs warns: "Bread of deceit is sweet to a man; but afterwards his mouth shall be filled with gravel."

7. Credibility is key. It is earned or lost through past and present performance and reputation. Take good care of it. Credibility is a valuable asset.

8. Silence and body language can be as significant as words and deeds. Be careful of what you don't say and do as you are of what you do say and do.

9. As the Bible tells us: "To everything there is a season, and a time to every purpose under the heaven" including "a time to keep silence, and a time to speak; a time to love, and a time to hate; a time of war, and a time of peace." This is also true of a negotiation.

10. Bear in mind the Bible's admonition: "A wrathful man stirreth up strife, but he that is slow to anger appeaseth strife."

MEDIATION

Mediation is similar to negotiation, except it involves the addition of one or more neutral mediators who work to facilitate communication and understanding between the parties. A mediator helps the parties explore various solutions to their differences, but the parties retain control of the results and are not obligated to follow the mediator's advice.[26]

Conflict resolution theories must be utilized if the mediator is to be successful in mediating. The mediator must implement all the basic skills of mediation and integrate into the session what is best for the client; plus, design a plan that will work in the future for the relationship on both sides. The mediator has to have skills to facilitate settlement between the parties.

This paper will explore ways to enhance the mediation process through an overlay of communication techniques designed to facilitate the effectiveness of the mediator, thereby creating an expanded communication environment for the parties.

Much is written on the process of mediation, or the sequences in the mediation process; however, little has been published on innovative approaches that the mediator can utilize during mediation to enhance the process. The ability to effectively deal with conflict is a life skill that everyone should possess. It is the researcher's goal to bring an understanding of the mediation process and techniques to as many people and their families as possible.

---

26 Sande, 213.

TEN COMMANDMENTS FOR MEDIATORS

1. Remember: your goal is to get the disputants to agree with each other; it is not to pass judgment on the merits of their respective claims.

2. Never let your personal views on the merits of the dispute influence your mediation efforts.

3. It is not inappropriate and is, in fact, desirable for you to take control of the "housekeeping" or such procedural aspects of the dispute as where and when the meetings should be held, how long they should last and whether and when public statements should be issued to the media.

4. Emphasize at the outset the importance of clearly defining the issues in dispute and gathering and assessing the relevant facts.

5. Carefully avoid any statements or actions that might prejudice the bargaining position of either side.

6. Make no recommendations for settlement unless specifically asked t do so by both sides and even then bear in mind that your ability to continue mediating may be prejudiced if one side accepts your recommendations and the other side rejects them.

7. You may, however, offer suggestions providing you make clear that you are advancing them simply for discussion and not as a recommended solution.

8. Convey accurately any messages or proposals either side relays through you and honor and respect any confidences you are given.

9. Never go around the individuals designated by each side as their spokespersons; as the Bible says, "accuse not a servant to his master."

10. Keep in mind at all times that the measure of your success depends entirely on your ability to get both sides to agree with each other.

The specific techniques that will be overlaid on the mediation process are: mirroring, anchoring, communication tracking, and numerous applications of how parties mentally process new and old information. During the mediation process, there are many opportunities to apply these techniques.

The mirroring process is useful to align the parties and the mediator. This non verbal communication process allows the mediator to be one with the presenter, because she sees and hears the same facial expressions, speech patterns, body position, as herself from the presenter. The mediator can calm, relax, sooth, or in other positive ways, modify any non-productive behavior or speech.

Anchoring is another useful technique to use during the core of the mediation process. It allows the mediator to use a positive verbal or non-verbal action when the parties are communicating in a forward fashion.

Types of anchors most frequently used are a positive nod, an appropriate wink, a permitted touch on the arm, and a gesture of the body or hand that makes a parentheses around a statement. A mediator must be extremely careful not to use an anchor to emphasize negative behaviors or attitudes of parties, nor to create a power imbalance, or appearance of non-neutrality between the parties.

With communication tracking, tracking the parties communication level is important throughout all aspects of the process. Parties operate on various levels of communication. These can be from a basic command level up to a free spirited one. Where they are and where they are coming from is essential to know in order to direct the process.

We, as people, have that natural tendency to want to resolve conflicts. One of the most important aspects of the mechanics of conflict resolution concerns authority. The parties in the dispute must possess the authority to make or effectively recommend decisions that can become binding. Attempts to resolve a conflict will not be successful if both parties do not have the authority to reach an agreement to resolve their dispute.

Mediation is a process of resolving disputes in which the parties involved and a trained, neutral mediator will work toward a mutually agreeable solution. Innocence and guilt are not decided. Satisfactory solution is the goal to reach.

The most typical situations involve issues between friends, neighbors, roommates, divorcing couples, landlords and tenants. Large corporations are also finding great savings in mediating their disputes. In our today conflict, we are finding more and more applications of mediation as a form of dispute resolution. Mediation works when those involved are committed to resolving their differences.

Communication is the key to resolving disputes. Each person in a dispute has something to contribute to the solution; it is possible for all persons involved in a dispute to emerge as winners.

Alternative dispute resolution was used as the first alternative to court, because attorneys and the court system were not trusted by citizens. However, these courts were used as the last resort. Arbitration, the oldest form, was traditionally used in commercial suits. The results were binding or non-binding, depending upon the contract between the parties who submitted to the process under Title 7, Chapter 154, which encouraged settlement of civil suits, moderated settlement conferences, summary jury trials, mini trials, arbitration and mediation. In the criminal area, mediation is the only method currently authorized by law and used by criminal courts and community dispute resolution centers.

To-date, most mediations have been civil in nature, due to the history of alternative dispute resolution in this country. It was only natural to revive civil mediations as an alternative to the crowded courts in a community setting with the addition of the local dispute resolution centers. With the exception of a few mediated restitution agreements, the civil side of our justice system has enjoyed the use of alternative dispute resolution in alleviating their crowded dockets. In the late seventies, both federal and state courts enacted legislation which embraced alternative dispute resolution as a method of relieving congested dockets at the initial and appellate level.

Mediation differs from arbitration in that the mediator is a neutral third party who does not impose an arbitration award, but only facilitates communication and negotiation between the parties. Another way mediation differs from all other forms of alternative dispute resolution is more emphasis is put on facilitation than on settlement. In the mediation model, the emphasis is put on the mediation process. The mediator does not have the authority to decide any issue for the parties, but will attempt to facilitate the voluntary resolution of the dispute by the parties. The parties understand that the mediator will not and cannot impose a settlement in their case, and agree that they are responsible for negotiating a settlement acceptable to them.

The mediator can fix the time of each mediation session. The sessions are private; the parties and their representatives may attend mediation sessions. Other persons may attend only with the permission of the parties and with the consent of the mediator. All information disclosed to a mediator shall be confidential. The parties shall maintain the confidentiality of the mediation and shall not rely on, or introduce as evidence in any arbitral, judicial, or other proceeding.

No subpoenas, summons, complaints, citations, writs or other process may be served upon any person at or near the site of any mediation session. Any person entering, attending, or leaving the session should not be encumbered with such.

Mediation is growing rapidly in popularity. Some see it as the wave of the future in conflict prevention and resolution. Understanding the values of mediation and how it works, the number of disputes that can be resolved with the help of mediation can be increased. Mediation is growing, and can do no harm. The exceptions are few in number, but it is important to know what they are.

Confidentiality of the discussions, which are in the nature of settlement talks, must be fully protected. The mediator's lips must be sealed and the parties themselves must agree that no reference to any proposals they make can be used in any other forum.

A mediator is simultaneously an educator and a housekeeper. He clarifies the issues, helps gather and assess the relevant facts, suggests lines of inquiry that might be fruitful, arranges for meetings and determines how long they should last, also exchanges messages and keeps the negotiations from lapsing into disarray. A mediator is a negotiator with a special purpose. The goal is to get the negotiators to agree with each other. Also, their goal is to get the other side to agree to give them what they want.

Mechanics of conflict prevention and resolution in mediation, nonetheless, are much the same as in negotiation. Found in the mediator's is the difference in design and execution of strategies and tactics to achieve his goal of getting the disputants to agree with each other. Focusing on the goal of joint agreement, a negotiator is well equipped to serve as a mediator in other disputes. Appropriate strategies and tactics follow from a clear understanding of the goal of a mediator.

In helping the parties reach an agreement, the mediator has served his purpose. However, he may not always succeed. But even in failure, it is unlikely that he will do harm. Mediation is an art, not a science. Its conduct varies with the skills and personalities of the mediators and the effectiveness of their efforts. John (Tex) McCrary, the noted publicist, described mediators as catalysts on a hot tin roof. The dictionary defines catalyst as an agent that causes activities between two or more agents without being affected by the action. A mediator is never a party to the ultimate agreement. He can be disappointed or overjoyed by the outcome, but he is not personally affected by agreement or disagreement.[27]

A disputant who proposes mediation is saying he is willing to give more or to accept less. The most serious obstacle to the introduction of mediation occurs at the moment when it can be most helpful, in the event of an impasse in negotiations. If the person is not prepared to make any change, there is no purpose to mediation. To accept mediation, however, sometimes is seen by the other party as a sign of weakness, an indication of a lack of bargaining strength to get what they want through negotiation. But this obstacle can be overcome by a third party proposing mediation, as well as being done by someone whose word is respected. Cardinal O'Connor proposed mediation in a dispute between television engineers and technicians and their network, and it worked.[28] Dispute parties can anticipate at the

---

27   PERC 101: Module 10, 2.
28   Ibid., 3.

beginning of their negotiations that their disputes could arise in the future and provide for their mediation or arbitration.

A disputant can more easily propose arbitration without appearing to weaken his bargaining position. He might say he is willing to have a third party pass judgement on its merits, whether he means it or not. There are other ways in which mediation can be introduced without compromising the bargaining position of either side. It may be difficult for the parties themselves to evoke mediation, and they may say they do not believe mediation can serve a purpose, but they will not object if it is proposed.

A history of frustration, these are neighborhood disputes that often fall into a gray area of issues that are too bothersome to ignore, but momentarily too insignificant to take to court. Anyone who has ever dealt with this type of dispute recognizes how complex they may become.

Community mediation in the United States is as old as the pilgrims. All disputes were settled within the community to foster unity and strength; however, if the individual did not comply with the community sanction, they were physically cast out and isolated. The community maintained order and peace among its citizens via shared community values. As shared community values gave way to individual rights in the civil law arena, and the state assuming the victim role in the criminal area, community mediation as a concept decreased. Therefore, today community mediation is increasing as a viable alternative, due to crowded court dockets and the workload of the courtroom work group.

In a 1906 speech titled "The Causes of Popular Dissatisfaction with the Administration of Justice," Harvard Law School Dean Roscoe Pound suggested that while discontent is inherent in any democratic legal system, much of the problem results from the way the system resolves disputes. He said America is simply behind the times and that much of the disgruntlement with the court processes was unnecessary.[29]

---

29   Randolph Lowry, and Richard W. Meyers, Conflict Management and Counseling. Volume 29 of the Resources for Christian Counseling series. Copyright by Word, Inc., 216.

In 1986, the California Legislature enacted the California dispute Resolution Programs Act to encourage more effective and efficient dispute resolution through greater use of alternatives to the courts, such as mediation, conciliation, and arbitration. Under this act, revenues to fund local, non-court dispute-resolution programs are being collected in over one-third of California's counties, which have voluntarily decided to participate. These programs provide a wide range of dispute-resolution services, including mediation, conciliation, and arbitration.

These programs can trace their roots back to the Los Angeles Neighborhood Justice Center which, in 1978, was one of the three federally funded pilot projects that provided the community with mediation services. Also in the same year, the first in a series of California legislative proposals promoting community alternative dispute resolution was passed.

In 1986, the Dispute Resolution Programs Act encouraged courts, law enforcement agencies, prosecuting authorities, and administrative agencies to make greater use of alternative dispute resolution techniques. This expansion should result in a well developed and effective system of community dispute resolution programs in every county by the year 2000.[30] Both the community based programs and the multi-door courthouse projects provide dispute-resolution services for neighbors, family members, landlords and tenants, employers and employees, and merchants and customers.

The District of Columbia Mediation Services are community based programs. This center will screen five times as many cases as the cases that are actually mediated. Many, as the serious criminal cases, are rejected as inappropriate for mediation. Many disputes will come to agreement. Almost 80% result in written agreements, and 75% to 80% of the people indicate the agreements were maintained. Most of the cases take less than two hours to resolve.[31]

Neighborhood centers are serving fairly specific communities and problems using mediation. The Martin Luther King Resolution Center, located in the African American, Latino, and Asian communities of

---

30   Ibid., 218.
31   Ibid., 219.

South Central Los Angeles, Director Dennis Westbrook feels the center's services are fulfilling King's philosophy of empowering the community, through nonviolence, a process which affirms justice, equality, and individual dignity.

Westbrook states, when we educate people about what alternative dispute resolution offers, people can take responsibility for their own disputes and reconcile themselves. Affirming nonviolence is the only reasonable way to empower a community.[32]

The mediator's goal is to process from a past centered approach to a future centered approach. Disputants will often start with harsh denunciations, or can be politely withdrawn, followed by venting emotions, reframing the disputants view of the conflict from a negative experience to a more neutral challenge, problem solving and a final decision.

The process will have to build basic trust, first in the mediator, then in the opponent. The trust will build from the disputants being listened to, and this could be for the first time. The mediator can convey the idea of respect and protection; this can show solutions to small points of disagreement. They can then transfer the energy they have been putting into self defense into problem solving.[33]

In her 1986 book, Peacemaking in Your Neighborhood, Jennifer Beer relates, "A mediator's description of the moment when the mediation's energy begins to change from negative to positive."[34]

In the last several years, one of the great developments is the involvement of Christian conciliation service programs. The programs were developed in the beginning to represent the church as a resource for dispute resolution. However, they have broadened their definitions of ministry to individuals who may not profess any particular spiritual commitment. Each year, hundreds of disputants are assisted by this service of Christian mediators and many are touched by the spirit of Christ. Community dispute resolution programs can be a valuable resource for the church, as well as for individual Christians.

---

32   Ibid., 220-221.
33   Ibid., 221.
34   Ibid.

Harvard University President Derek Bok predicts society's greatest opportunities will lie in tapping inclinations toward collaboration and compromise, rather than stirring our proclivities for competition and rivalry.[35]

Mediation is a biblical idea. It is the essence of the gospel of Jesus Christ. In I Timothy 2:5-6, Paul wrote: "For there is one God and one mediator between God and men, the man Christ Jesus, who gave Himself as a ransom for all men, the testimony given in its proper time."

A simple translation for the word mediation is in the middle. A mediator is someone who places himself/herself in the middle of conflict in bringing about some kind of resolution of a problem in hope of some reconciliation between people.

Whatever circumstance exists, the mediator will find the seven basic stages in the mediation process, listed in the following table.[36]

SEVEN STAGES
OF THE MEDIATION PROCESS

1. Prepare for mediation

2. Begin the mediation session

3. Communicate about the dispute

4. Define the issues and set the agenda

5. Clarify information and uncover hidden interests

6. Generate and assess options for settlement

7. Bring session to disclosure and settlement

---

3 Table 9-1

---

35   Ibid., 227.
36   Ibid., 108.

Games theory provides a useful means of relating and distinguishing negotiation, mediation, arbitration and litigation from each other. The theory divides games into three categories: skill, chance, and strategy; and identifies them by their dominant characteristics. Skill of the competitors determines who will be the winner.

In games of strategy, the best course of action for each player depends on what the other players do. The focus is on the players decisions and their actions. In games theory, the play-off, or outcome, is measured by what is known as the value system of each player. In zero sum games, there is a winner and loser. If one side wins, it is clear that the other side has lost.

In variable sum games, the outcome is separately measured by each side in light of their respective objectives. This can produce two winners, two losers, or a winner and a loser.

Mediation and negotiation are variable sum games. A successful negotiation can have two winners. A buyer could be happy with his acquisition while the seller might be satisfied with the price he has been paid. An employer who gains productivity improvements may view himself as a winner; an employee who obtained an increase in pay in exchange, may be satisfied with his raise. Mediation and negotiation can produce two losers or two winners and one loser.

In the parlance of games theory, the parties in an ongoing relationship can have mixed motives, cooperation in achieving a company's profits and over their distribution.

The mediator is not a necessary or proper party in judicial proceedings relating to the mediation. Neither mediator nor any law firm employing a mediator shall be liable to any party for any act or omission in connection with any mediation conducted under these rules, and they are indemnified and held harmless for any loss, cost, or expense.

The mediator's daily fee should be agreed upon prior to mediation. He/she should be paid in advance of each mediation day.

A mediator may not impose his own judgement on the issues for that of the parties.[37]

ARBITRATION

Arbitration has the advantage of being very economical. The cost of an arbitration is far lower than any court action. Arbitration has already saved Americans hundreds of millions of dollars in lawsuit costs.

Arbitration is not a mystery; parties can handle their own cases. Arbitration decisions are made and enforced in every jurisdiction. The United States supreme Court has ruled that properly prepared arbitration agreements are always enforceable. The prevailing party may be awarded costs, encouraging valid cases and discouraging spurious claims.

Arbitration is efficient. Decisions are returned in weeks, not years. Justice is not delayed, and not denied.[38] Arbitration provides advantages for every contracting party and potential litigant. Unlike the lawsuit system, which emphasizes process and a war of attrition, arbitration provides prompt, rational decisions.

Arbitration allows consumers to recover both damages and costs of process. It provides prompt, rational and inexpensive results, with the cost commensurate with the issues. Many employers and employees have used arbitration and mediation for decades with efficient, rational processes benefitting all parties. Prompt decisions allow both parties to get on with jobs, tasks, and business. Costs, both monetary and in time, are related to real issues, with the prevailing party recovering the cost.

The future of arbitration is now. In the past 18 months, the United States Supreme court has issued far reaching opinions favoring uniformity in arbitration-holding that, for all matters involving interstate commerce, the Federal Arbitration Act preempts state laws that attempt to regulate arbitration. This means that every industry

---

37   Craig a. McEwen (1987), "Differing Visions of alternative Dispute Resolution and Formal Law," The Justice System Journal, 12, 247=259.

38   "Why Arbitrate?", 1-10.

involving interstate commerce-banking and finance, health care, transportation, literally every type of business-can draft one standard arbitration clause and use arbitration in a uniform way throughout the United States.[39]

Supreme Court decisions mean something else. The highest court in the land supports the use of quick, inexpensive arbitration for all types of disputes. Hundreds of lower court opinions have followed suit.[40]

"The courts of this country should not be the places where the resolution of disputes begins. They should be the places where disputes end, after alternative methods of resolving disputes have been considered and tried."[41]

Authority of Arbitrators, Rule 35, [42] arbitrators have the powers provided by this code, the agreement of the parties, and the law. Arbitrators shall take an oath, prescribed by the Director, that is neutral and independent. Arbitrators decide all issues submitted by the parties and do not have the power to decide matters not properly submitted under this code. Arbitrators may grant any remedy of relief allowed by applicable substantive law and based on a claim, response or request properly submitted by a party under this code.[43]

Appointment of Arbitrators, Rule 21, the Director appoints the arbitrators to conduct hearings and shall establish qualifications and compensation for arbitrators. The Director provides written notice to all parties of the name and qualifications of an arbitrator at least fifteen (15) days before the date specified for the hearing. In the case of an expedited hearing, the appointment of the arbitrator shall accompany notice of the hearing. In an arbitration involving parties who are citizens of or which have their principle places of business in different countries, the Director shall appoint an arbitrator who is a citizen of a country other than that of the parties, unless the agreement of the parties provide otherwise.

---

39   Ibid.
40   Ibid., 4 of 10.
41   Ibid., 9 of 10.
42   ADR Code of Procedure, Rule 20.
43   Ibid., 1 of 2.

Number of arbitrators, Rule 22, states for all participatory hearings where the amount of any claim is less than one-million United States dollars ($1,000,000) and for all document hearings the Director shall appoint one (1) arbitrator, unless the parties agree to more arbitrators. For all other participatory hearings, the Director shall appoint an arbitration panel consisting of three (3) arbitrators unless the parties agree otherwise, and shall select the Chair of the panel.[44]

Disqualification of arbitrator, Rule 23, conveys that an arbitrator shall be disqualified if circumstances exist that create a conflict of interest or cause the arbitrator to be unfair and biased.[45] One such disqualifying circumstance would be if an arbitrator has a personal bias or prejudice concerning a party, or personal knowledge of disputed evidentiary facts. Another would be if the arbitrator has served as an attorney to any party, the arbitrator has been associated with an attorney who has represented a party during that association, or the arbitrator or an associated attorney is a material witness concerning the matter before the arbitrator. If he/she, individually or as a fiduciary, or the arbitrator's spouse or minor child residing in the arbitrator's household, has a direct financial interest in a matter before the arbitrator, he/she is risking disqualification. Still another disqualifying circumstance would be if the arbitrator, or the arbitrator's spouse, or a person within the third degree of relationship to either of them, or the spouse of such a person, is either a party to the proceeding, or an officer, director, or trustee of a party; or, is acting as a lawyer in the proceeding.

An arbitrator shall disclose to the director circumstances that create a conflict of interest or cause an arbitrator to be unfair and biased. The director shall disqualify an arbitrator or shall inform the parties of information disclosed by the arbitrator if the arbitrator is not disqualified.[46]

A party may challenge the appointment of an arbitrator by filing with the Director a written request stating the circumstances and

---

44   ADR Code of Procedure, 1 of 2.
45   Ibid.
46   Ibid., 2 of 2.

specific reasons for the disqualification. The request to challenge must be received by the Director no later than ten (10) days after the challenging party receives notice of the appointment of the arbitrator.[47]

Therefore, the Director shall promptly review the challenge and determine whether circumstances exist requiring disqualification in accord with Rule 23A.[48] However, if an arbitrator becomes unable to arbitrate before the issuance of an award, the Director shall appoint a new arbitrator or panel and reschedule the hearing, unless the parties agree otherwise.[49]

In Communications with Arbitrator, Rule 24, parties shall not communicate with an arbitrator except at a Participatory Hearing or by providing documents in accord with this code, or with the permission of the Director who may permit, for sufficient reason, a conference with the arbitrator and all the parties.[50]

One way to ensure that conflict is related to contract relationships will be resolved in a biblical manner rather than in court is to include a conciliation clause in the contract itself. The Institute for Christian Conciliation recommends using a clause like this. Any claim or dispute arising out of, or relating to this agreement, shall be settled by mediation and, if necessary, arbitration in accordance with the Rules of Procedure for Christian Conciliation of the Institute for Christian Conciliation. Any judgment upon an arbitration award may be entered in any court of competent jurisdiction.

The Institute of Christian Conciliation has developed a set of forms, guidelines, and procedures that can be used by church leaders and others when they are serving as conciliators or arbitrators.[51]

In arbitration the parties agree to present each side of their dispute before one or more neutral arbitrators. Unlike mediators, arbitrators do not attempt to help the parties communicate with each other or assist in negotiating a settlement. Instead, like judges,

---

47   Ibid.
48   Ibid.
49   Ibid.
50   Ibid.
51   Ken Sande, The Peacemaker, 9th Printing, Scripture quotations are from the New International Version, U.S.A.: Zondervan Bible Publisher, 1996, 232.

they gather evidence and render a binding decision. Most states have laws that allow parties to appoint their own arbitrators; these may be volunteers.

The advantage of arbitration when compared to negotiation and mediation is that it always produces a resolution to a dispute, even if one or both parties are unhappy. However, in contrast to litigation, arbitration is private and informal and most of the time less expensive, and produces a final legally result more quickly.

When compared to negotiation and mediation, the disadvantage of arbitration is that relationship problems are ignored, which often perpetrates or aggravates personal estrangement. Arbitration has disadvantages when compared to litigation. It is less guarded by procedural rules. Because many arbitrators lack formal legal training, arbitrated decisions are sometimes less consistent and predictable than those that would result in a court of law. If one party refuses to abide by the arbitrator's decision, the other party may still need to resort to the courts to enforce it.[52]

Christian Conciliation may involve three steps. First, one or both parties may receive individual counseling on how to resolve the dispute in private. Second, if private efforts are unsuccessful, the parties may submit their dispute for mediation, a process in which one of more Christian conciliators meet with them to promote constructive dialogue and to encourage a voluntary and biblically faithful settlement of their differences Third, if mediation is unsuccessful, the parties may proceed to arbitration, which means that one or more arbitrators will hear their case and render a biblical and legally binding decision.[53]

Christian conciliation does have limitations, however. They do not have the same authority as civil judges and therefore cannot force parties to cooperate with conciliation or abide by the results. Signed agreement reached through mediation and arbitration awards can be enforced by a civil court.[54] Ideally, Christian conciliation should

---

52   Ibid., 213.
53   Sande, 214.
54   Ibid., 215.

be pursued within a local church with the help of spiritually mature Christians.

A good arbitrator is not necessarily a good mediator. Frequently, he is focused on the merits of the opposing claims. This is a virtue in arbitration. In mediation, it can detract from the goal of getting both sides to agree with each other.

Christian conciliation is a process for reconciling persons and resolving disputes out of court in a biblically faithful manner. It encourages honest communication and reasonable cooperation, rather than unnecessary contention and manipulation. Christian conciliation usually provides more thorough and satisfying solutions to conflict than can be obtained through secular processes.

TEN COMMANDMENTS FOR ARBITRATORS

1. Keep in mind that: your goal is to decide the dispute in accordance with the mandate the parties have given you; it is not to impose your judgment of fairness. Simply splitting the difference is a cop-out.

2. If the dispute involves the rights of the parties under a contract, guide yourself by the contract's terms which usually limit you to an interpretation and application of the contract. You have no authority to add to, subtract from, or modify its terms.

3. If interest claims are involved, guide yourself by the criteria in the stipulation of the parties submitting the dispute to arbitration.

4. While the atmosphere surrounding an arbitration is usually less severe than in a courtroom, you are the final decision-maker and you should conduct yourself as a judge would but without the black robes or elevated presence.

5. It is not good form to speak to one party in the absence of the other side even on matters unrelated to the arbitration; it is especially bad form if the matter has to do with the arbitration.

6. If the opportunity arises, you may wish to try to mediate. But neither say or do anything in mediation that might prejudice your ability to make a decision on the merits.

7. Your decision and opinion should be confined to the case before you. You should not include any incidental or supplementary remarks.

8. You should not allow anyone unconnected with the arbitration to be present in the hearing without the consent of both sides.

9. Your decision and opinion should not be made public without the consent of both sides.

10. You should agree with both parties in advance on the terms of your compensation. After an award, this may prove more difficult.

4PERC101: Module 12.

LITIGATION

Litigation is a form of conflict resolution. However, it deserves some attention because all four of the main methods of conflict resolution-negotiation, mediation, arbitration, and litigation-should be considered as part of a total approach to resolving conflict. As litigation is always an alternative to negotiation, mediation and arbitration in regard to rights disputes. Litigation has been around for many decades and has been the subject of intense study by scholars and practitioners here and abroad. The threat of litigation is an incentive for disputants to resolve their differences through negotiation, or to submit them to mediation or arbitration.

Litigation utilizes the judges, juries, and procedural rules of the civil court system. Litigation has several advantages compared to other methods of resolving a dispute. A court has the authority to require all parties to appear and to abide by its decisions. A court is able to render more predictable decisions on many issues with its foundation of statutes and case law.

Litigation has many disadvantages. In addition to being expensive and time consuming, litigation is constrained by formal procedures, encourages public attention, will offer limited remedies, money or injunctions, and allows one party to win completely while the other party loses everything. Court technicalities restrict understanding communication, often leaving the parties frustrated and angry. A court is usually forced to deal with the symptoms of a problem rather than its real causes, thus leaving the parties in an ongoing state of antagonism. As a result, litigation is likely to increase bitterness between the parties and further damage any personal relationship they had previously enjoyed.

Since every conflict is unique, one cannot address every question that might arise when a matter may be headed toward court. One way to apply these answers is to remember that you are a steward of Christ and to ask yourself, would my Master be pleased and honored if I use my time and resources to pursue this matter in court?[55]

From a spiritual perspective, the side affects of litigation is even more serious than any other secular methods of conflict resolution.[56] It obstructs confession and repentance, thus prolonging destructive habit patterns. As the hearts are hardened by these factors, they are likely to experience more conflict in the future. Justice Antonio Scalia said: "Judges can also tell you of brothers and sisters permanently estranged by litigation over a will, or of once friendly neighbors living in undying enmity because of a boundary dispute that is, in financial terms, inconsequential. Whatever the legal rights and wrongs of such matters, these results are not worth it."[57]

The first loss of those who turn to the litigation process is financial. Taxpayers also are called upon to financially support the public judicial system that provides this option for dispute resolution. Taxpayers pay a large amount of dollars each year for the courtrooms, the judges, and in some cases, the lawyers. Christians are often times involved in this burgeoning amount of litigation that is pushing the costly legal system into ever increasing expansion.

We also have lost emotionally when engaged in litigation. This can go on for years, with the anger and emotion put into it. Regardless of who won, friends are lost; participants are tired and spiritually drained.

The most serious loss incurred when conflict among Christians result in litigation, may be the church's loss of reputation as a community of believers. Sex scandals and financial scams are the most serious injuries to the church's reputation. One who engages in litigation has lost the ability to minister to others.

When we take someone to court, we have lost financially and emotionally. The church has lost its reputation, and Christ has lost our ministry.

Professor Frank A.E. Sander, of Harvard Law School, noted that courts were inundated with pending litigation. He suggested that

---

55   Ibid., 217.
56   Ibid., 213.
57   Ibid., 214.

many disputes could and should be resolved outside of court through processes of alternative dispute resolution. Sander proposed that by the year 2000, courthouses should no longer be arenas merely for litigation, but that they should become dispute-resolution centers offering mediation, arbitration and a variety of other problem-solving methods.[58]

In the mid 1970s, criminal courts and prosecutors in some cities were already experimenting with community dispute settlement in relation to minor crimes between people who had continuing relationships. The purpose of these early programs in Philadelphia, Columbus, New York, Rochester, and Boston was to substitute negotiation and restitution for prosecution by the state.[59] In 1978, United States Attorney General Griffin Bell established three neighborhood justice centers in Atlanta, Kansas City, and Los Angeles. The centers were to provide citizens with a local, grassroots, decentralized forum for dispute resolution and other legal services. During the 1980s, the three experimental neighborhood justice centers increased to more than 400 community based dispute-resolution programs.

Avoidance

Often overlooked, yet almost always available, is the response of avoidance. As used here, avoidance is not seen as the suppression or denial of conflict.[60] Jethro Lieberman suggests that as a society we have moved away from any acceptance of wrong to a circumstance where virtually any act by another is actionable.[61]

Conflict avoidance may be one alternative to this. Christ avoided conflict in a deliberate way. Often when the crowds were pressing, sometimes clamoring for miracles, he retreated to the hills and in doing so, diminished the escalation of the crowd's demands.[1] In the

---

58   Ibid.
59   Ibid., 217.
60   L. Randolph Lowry, J.D. Richard, and W. Meyers, Conflict Management and Counseling. Volume 29, United States of America, 1991.
61   Ibid.

Garden of Gethsemane, when he could have rallied not only his disciples but literally called down angels from heaven, Christ told Peter to put away his sword.[2] Finally, as Jesus anticipated His return to Jerusalem, it was obvious that He delayed that return, again avoiding what he understood would be great conflict.[3] Christ did not avoid but rather addressed his conflict with the money changers at the temple.[4] The apostles did not avoid but rather addressed the conflict over the Jewish insistence on Gentile circumcision through the Jerusalem Conference.[5] Paul did not avoid but rather dealt with his conflict concerning John Mark prior to his second missionary journey.[6]

While there are disputes that need the formality of courtroom litigation, in most cases it is neither necessary from a dispute resolution perspective or appropriate from a Christian perspective. The use of litigation is usually the result of an angry reaction without the awareness of better alternatives, and that both sides are not capable or have the desire to resolve their own dispute.[62]

---

62   Ibid. 53-54.

chapter three

RATIONALE FOR ESTABLISHING CONFLICT RESOLUTION PROGRAMS THROUGH NEGOTIATION, MEDIATION, AND CONSENSUS

Safe and orderly environments in our nation's schools are important to promoting high standards for learning and ensuring that all children have the opportunity to develop to their fullest potential. No teacher should ever have to fear walking into a classroom, and no child should ever stay home from school because he/she is afraid. However, too often young people face conflicts before, during, and after school. They are subjected to bullying, teasing, and senseless, sometimes fatal disputes over clothing and other possessions. Conflicts may begin at school or be brought into school from home or community.

Adults are not powerless to prevent these destructive behaviors. By providing young people with the knowledge and skills needed to settle disputes peacefully with conflict resolution education, significant reductions in suspensions, disciplinary referrals, academic disruptions, playground fights, and family and sibling disputes can result.

Conflict resolution education is a critical component of comprehensive, community based efforts to prevent violence and reduce crime.

As adults, we cannot solve young people's problems for them. However, we can provide knowledge, skills, and encouragement to resolve conflicts in a nonviolent manner, using words instead of fists or weapons. When problem solving processes to conflict and strife become a way of life, young people begin to value getting along instead of getting even or getting their way. Conflict resolution education includes negotiation, mediation, and consensus decision making, which allows all parties involved a peaceful solution to a conflict, working together in the schools, community organizations, and other youth-serving and juvenile justice settings to give youths the skills, techniques, and tools they need to learn and to resolve disputes in a safe and nonviolent environment.[63]

We have a juvenile justice system that in many states is bankrupt and is starting too late. You cannot start with a 16 or 17 year old who has dropped out of school and who was the drug dealer's gofer by the time he was age 13. We must start earlier. We can do tremendous amounts of good through conflict resolution programs in our public schools.[64]

---

63   S.B. Goldberg, and H.J. Reske, "Talking with Attorney General Janet Reno," American Bar Association Journal, 1993, 79:46.
64   Ibid.

PURPOSES OF CONFLICT
RESOLUTION EDUCATION

American schools must first be safe places. Our schools are challenged to provide an environment in which each learner can feel physically and psychologically free from threats and danger and can find opportunities to work and learn with others for the mutual achievement of all. The diversity of the school's population is respected and celebrated to fulfill their mission of educating youth and preparing them to function effectively in adult society.

Conflict resolution programs can help schools promote both the individual behavioral change necessary for responsible citizenship and the systemic change necessary for a safe learning environment. Schools can be places for children to learn to live in civil association with one another and prepare for their future roles as parents, community members and leaders, as well as productive people of the workforce. With the ability to resolve disputes effectively and nonviolently is the peaceful expression of human rights. Conflict resolution can be viewed as a responsibility of law-abiding members of our society. Building good relationships with citizens is most important in showing and shaping how people choose to disagree.[65]

We can learn new habits of mind. It is not too late for a paradigm shift in our outlook toward human conflict. Education can be turned into a force for reducing intergroup conflict. It can emphasize common characteristics and goals and broaden our understanding of diverse cultures, even in circumstances of conflict.

Cultural conflicts are based on differences in national origin or ethnicity. Many conflicts in our schools will arise out of differences. Social conflicts are based on differences in gender, sexual orientation, class, and physical and mental abilities.

---

65 T. Amsler, (March), "Educating for Citizenship: Reframing Conflict Resolution Work in K-12 Schools." Paper presented at the Coulson Festshrift Meeting, Aspen Institute, Wye Conference Center, Queenstown, Maryland, March 13-14, 1994.

Education programs provide a framework for addressing these problems. The programs promote respect and acceptance with new ways of communicating and understanding.[66]

The best school-based violence prevention programs seek to do more than reach the individual child. Instead, they try to change the total school environment, to create a safe community that lives by a credo of nonviolence.[67]

The significant problems we face cannot be solved at the same level of thinking we were when we created them.[68] When youth experience success with negotiation, mediation, or consensus decision making in school or other youth serving settings, they are most likely to use these conflict resolution processes elsewhere in their lives.

Conflict resolution, when implemented not only as curriculum to be taught but as a lifestyle to be lived by both adults and youths, fosters continuous academic and social growth. The school programs can help create governance structures, develop policies, identify goals, make curriculum decisions, and plan for assessment of learning. Faculty and students can work and learn together while supporting one another. When this is practiced by all, respect, caring, tolerance, and community building becomes the way to do things akin to: teaching alternatives to violence; teaching students to act responsibility in social settings; and teaching students to understand and accept the consequences of behavior.[69]

A conflict resolution program provides an effective alternative to a traditional discipline program. Youth who grow up in circumstances in which they are socialized to violence, physical abuse, or even death will not be brought into submission by punishments such as lowered grades, time out, detention, suspension, or even expulsion. However, alternatives that will lead to long-term changes in attitudes and behavior are needed. Conflict resolution programs are an important

---

66   Ibid.
67   W. Delong, "School-Based Violence Prevention: From the Peaceable School to the Peaceable Neighborhood," Forum, 1994 (Spring) No. 25, 8.
68   D. Hamburg. Education for Conflict Resolution. Report of the President of the Carnegie Corporation of New York, p. 15.
69   Amsler, March 13-14, 1994.

part of those alternatives because of the participation to plan more effective behavior and then to behave accordingly.

The problem-solving processes of conflict resolution (negotiation, mediation, and consensus decision making) can improve the school climate. Conflict resolution strategics reduce violence, vandalism, chronic absence, and suspensions. Conflict resolution training helps students and teachers deepen their understanding of themselves and others and develops important life skills. Training in negotiation, mediation, and consensus decision making encourages a high level of citizenship activity. Conflict resolution training helps students and teachers to deepen their understanding of each other, as well as to develop important life skills. With this type of training, the problem solving processes of conflict resolution (negotiation, mediation, and consensus decision making) can improve the school climate. Also, with shifting the responsibility for solving nonviolent conflict to students, frees adults to concentrate more on teaching and less on discipline.[70]

Behavior management systems that are more effective than detention, suspension, or expulsion are needed to deal with conflict in the school settings. Conflict resolution training increases skills in listening, critical thinking, and problem solving skills basic to all learning. Negotiation and mediation are problem solving tools that are well suited to the problems that young people face, and those trained in these approaches often use them to solve problems for which they would not seek adult help.[71] Conflict resolution education emphasizes seeing other points of view and resolving differences peacefully-skills that assist one to live in a multi cultural world.

---

70   Hamburg, 15.
71   D. Hamburg, Education for Conflict Resolution, Report of the President of the Carnegie Corporation of New York, 1994, 15.

UNDERSTANDING CONFLICT RESOLUTION

Conflict arises from a discord of needs, drives, wishes, and/or demands. Conflict is not of itself positive or negative. It is the response to conflict that transforms it into either a competitive, destructive experience or a constructive challenge offering the opportunity for growth. Conflict is just part of life; learning how to respond to it constructively is needed. Developing an understanding of conflict resolution and the principles suggest that when limited resources are at issue, an individual's best interests lie in cooperation, not competing. Most all individuals are motivated by needs.[72]

Glasser identifies four basic psychological needs that motivate behavior:

1. **Belonging**: Fulfilled by loving, sharing and cooperating with others.
2. **Power**: Fulfilled by achieving, accomplishing, and being recognized and respected.
3. **Freedom**: Fulfilled by making choices.
4. **Fun**: Fulfilled by laughing and playing when conflict arises in a relationship, individuals have two choices, to continue the conflict or to problem solve. Basic psychological needs are at the root of almost all conflict.[73]

Secretary of Education, Richard W. Riley, suggests that learning can take place only when schools are safe, disciplined, and drug free. Schools in all types of communities, urban, rural, and suburban, are taking steps to be free of violent and disruptive behaviors. Secretary of Education Richard W. Riley suggests that incorporating conflict

---

72   W. Glasser, Control Theory. New York, NY: Harper & Row, 1984, 7.
73   Ibid.

resolution education into the curriculum can be an important step in ensuring a safe and healthy learning environment.[74]

If basic needs are not addressed along with the resource issue, conflicts over limited resources may not be resolved. However, the resource issue by itself may not define the problem. Therefore, conflict between the parties will likely occur again, mostly when solutions deal only with the limited resource that appears to be the source of the conflict without addressing other underlying interests.

Figure 1: Understanding Conflict

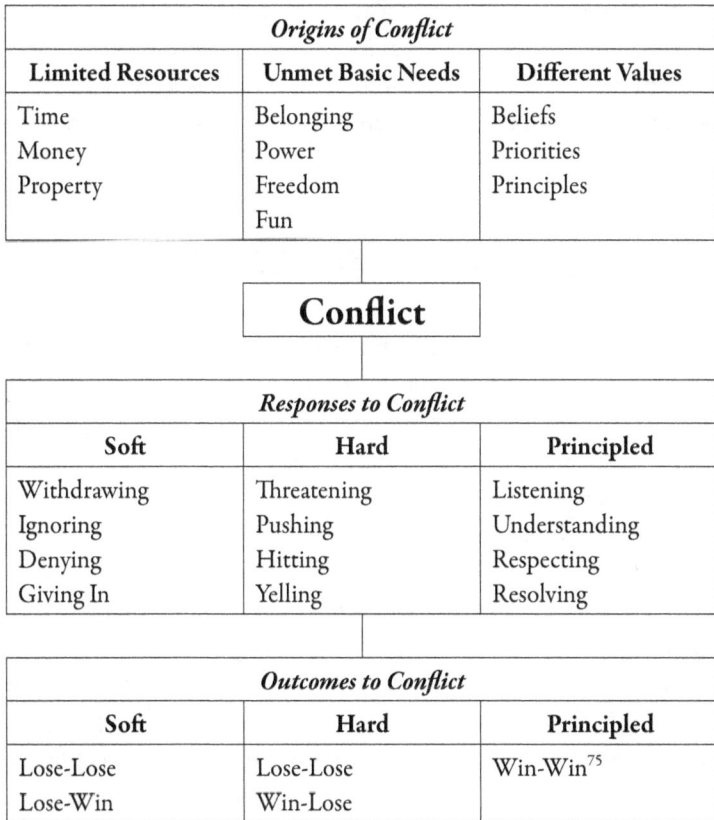

Origins of Conflict		
Limited Resources	**Unmet Basic Needs**	**Different Values**
Time	Belonging	Beliefs
Money	Power	Priorities
Property	Freedom	Principles
	Fun	

Conflict

Responses to Conflict		
Soft	**Hard**	**Principled**
Withdrawing	Threatening	Listening
Ignoring	Pushing	Understanding
Denying	Hitting	Respecting
Giving In	Yelling	Resolving

Outcomes to Conflict		
Soft	**Hard**	**Principled**
Lose-Lose	Lose-Lose	Win-Win[75]
Lose-Win	Win-Lose	

---

74 Ibid..
75 R.D. Bodine, and F. Schrumpf, Creating the Peaceable School: A Comprehensive Program for Teaching Conflict Resolution, Champaign, IL: Research Press, Inc., 1994, 92.

DIFFERENT VALUES

When an individual holds a value, he/she has an enduring belief that a specific action or quality is preferable to another action or quality. Conflicts involving different values, beliefs, priorities, or principles tend to be more difficult to resolve. Many times disputants think in terms of right/wrong or good/bad when values are in opposition.[76]

Values disputes may be rooted in issues of social diversity. Differences in cultural, social, physical, and mental attributes are often expressed as different beliefs, conviction, and/or principles. These conflicts can be resolved by increased awareness, understanding, and respect. Conflict rooted in prejudice or bias against another, ignorance, fear, and misunderstanding often guide behavior toward that person.[77]

RESPONSES TO CONFLICT

Soft responses, avoidance, accommodation, and compromise usually occur between individuals who are friends, or who want to be pleasant to each other because they will continue to have contact in the future.

In soft and hard responses, disputants take positions or stands relative to the problem. They negotiate these positions by trying either to avoid or to win a contest of wills. Soft and hard negotiations either bring about one-sided losses or demand one-sided gains.[78]

Hard responses to conflict occur between individuals who are adversaries and whose goal is victory. Hard responses to a conflict are characterized by involving force, threats, aggression, and anger; often searching for a single answer to the problem-the other side giving in. Frequently, hard negotiations apply pressure, trying to win a contest of wills by using bribery and punishments, such as withholding money, favors, and affection. Hard responses are detrimental to cooperation

---

76   Ibid., 9.
77   Ibid.
78   Goldberg and Reske, 46.

and relationships and often result in hostility, physical damage, and violence.[79]

Soft responses typically result in two types of outcomes. One gives in on their position for the sake of the relationship, with the result that no one's interests are met, a lose-lose outcome. One side accommodates the other, occurring in a lose-win outcome . In this situation, the individuals who avoid conflict by accommodating others loses because in the sense their basic needs are not acknowledged or met. Often, these individuals see themselves as victims and their relations with others suffer.

Hard responses also typically result in two types of outcomes. Win-lose outcomes occur when the more aggressive wins and the adversary loses. Conflict with hard responses often lead to a situation in which the desire to punish or get even provokes actions that harm themselves as well as their opponents. This results in a lose-lose outcome.

Principle responses to conflict typically lead to a win-win outcome. The interests and needs of each party in the dispute are met, using a problem-solving process. Based on principled negotiation theory, individuals in conflict come to consensus on a joint resolution. All problem-solving processes in conflict resolution are based on integrated negotiation theory.

Negotiation is a problem-solving process in which either the two parties in the dispute, or their representatives, meet fact to face to work together unassisted to resolve the dispute between the parties.[80]

Mediation is a problem-solving process in which the two parties in the dispute, or their representatives, meet face to face to work together to resolve the dispute assisted by a neutral third party called the mediator.

Consensus decision making is a group problem-solving process in which all of the parties in the dispute, or representatives of each party, collaborate to resolve the dispute by crafting a plan of action

---

79 A. Adler, "Implementing District-Wide Programs: If I Knew Then What I Know Now," The Fourth R, 57, 1995, 5.

80 P. Moore, and D. Batiste, "Preventing Youth Violence: Prejudice Elimination and Conflict Resolution Programs," Forum, No. 25, 18.

that all parties can and will support. This process may or may not be facilitated by a neutral party.

Separate people from the problem. By separating the issues, individuals come to see themselves as working side by side, attacking the problem, not each other.[81]

Conflict is a natural, vital part of life. When conflict is understood, it can become an opportunity to learn and create. The challenge for people in conflict is to apply the principles of creative cooperation in their human relationships.[82]

Focus on interests, not positions. Positions are things individuals decide they want, and interests are the underlying motivations behind the positions they take.[83]

Invent options for mutual gain. Disputants focus on identifying options for resolving the conflict without the pressure of reaching a decision. A brainstorming process is suggested to invent a wide range of options that can advance shared interests and creatively reconcile differing interests. To broaden their options, those in a dispute think about the problem in different ways and build upon the ideas presented.[84]

Using objective criteria insures that the agreement reflects some fair standard instead of the arbitrary will of either side. Using this technique means that neither party needs to give in to the other. Rather, they can defer to a fair solution where objective criteria are determined by disputants based on fair standards and fair procedures.[85]

The six steps in each problem-solving process are: (1) setting the stage, (2) gathering perspectives, (3) identifying interests, (4) creating options, (5) evaluating options, and (6) generating agreement.

The Programs for Young Negotiators (PYN), a process curriculum program developed by Jared Curhan, aims to teach individuals how to achieve their goals without violence. The foundation abilities of perception and thinking that are taught in negotiation courses help students learn that to satisfy their own interest, they must empathize

81   Ibid.
82   Bodine and Crawford.
83   Moore and Bastiste, 18.
84   Bodine and Crawford, 52-53.
85   Ibid.

with the interests of others. PYN has four components: negotiation curriculums, ongoing curriculum development and innovation, follow up opportunities, and teacher training with community involvement. During this training session, participants learn negotiation from negotiation professors and practicing negotiators.

After teachers begin teaching negotiation concepts, they will also continue with their own ongoing technical support.

"Have you not learned great lessons from those who braced themselves against you, and disputed the passage with you?" (Walt Whitman) The negotiation curriculum is based on seven basic elements of negotiation developed at Harvard Law School.

Figure 2: Seven Elements of Negotiation

Harvard Negotiation Project	Program for Young Negotiators
• **Communicate** unconditionally both ways.	• Understand their **perceptions** and communicate your own.
• Build a **relationship** in which you work side by side.	• Be **trustworthy** all the time and collaborate.
• Clarify everyone's underlying **interests**.	• Explore their underlying **interests**, as well as your own.
• Without commitment, generate **options** to meet the interests.	• **Brainstorm** options without criticizing each other.
• Find external standards of **legitimacy** by which to evaluate and improve options.	• Identify **fair reasons** for choosing options
• Think about the walk-away **alternatives** if no agreement is reached.	• Know your **backup plan**.
• Carefully draft terms that are better than the best alternatives. Then make **commitments**.	• **Package** options based on both of your interests.[86]

---

86 Adapted with permission from materials of the Harvard Negotiation Project, Harvard Law School, Cambridge, Massachusetts, and of the Program for Young Netotiators, Inc., Cambridge, Massachusetts.

The content of the Peace Education Foundation conflict resolution curriculum has five components:

1. Community building-establishing trust, exploring common interests, and respecting differences.
2. Understanding conflict-identifying conflict, the elements of conflict, escalation and de-escalation, and different conflict management styles.
3. Perception-understanding different points of view, enhancing empathy, and increasing tolerance.
4. Anger management-understanding the pros and cons of anger, anger triggers, and anger styles, increasing tolerance for frustration; and learning anger management plans.
5. Rules for fighting fair-learning the rules that provide a framework for appropriate behavior and the associated skills, identifying and focusing on the problem; attacking the problem, not the person; listening with an open mind; treating a person's feelings with respect; and taking responsibility for one's actions.

These rules are central to the Peace Education Foundation conflict resolution program because they are the principles of non-violent conflict resolution that promote a peaceful, disciplined environment. These rules are to replace ways of inappropriate behaviors that attack the dignity of others and escalate conflict, such as putting the other person down, being sarcastic, bringing up the past, hitting, not taking responsibility, getting even, not listening, and making excuses.

Once the rules are mastered, more sophisticated content and skills from the PEF components can be added to enhance student's social competency. These additional components include affirming self-identity, refusing peer pressure, acting in a self empowering way, dealing with bullies, establishing self-control, setting goals, acting with courage and conviction, understanding violence, having healthy relationships with boyfriends/girlfriends, and being a peacemaker.

Five strategies teachers use from the PEF conflict resolution curriculum include modeling, teaching students what to do and why, coaching, ecouraging, and delegating. In practicing model behavior, the goal is to let students know how, in real life, to use the rules for fighting fair and skills such as reflective listening, "I" statement, and problem solving. Coach, offer support, and encourage students to behave appropriately without depending on adults. Teachers delegate to teach, or coach, less experienced students thus allowing them to demonstrate their competence and acknowledge the value of habitual use of the skills.

Our partnership with the Peace Education Foundation has reduced the number of referrals and improved the classroom climate in our schools.[87] Schools report that, as the number of students and adults skilled in mediation increases in a school, the incidents of conflict in the school decreases.[88] Parent involvement in the support for a school based conflict resolution program is critical.

PEF conflict resolution components may be incorporated into traditional academic lessons. Specific PEF curriculum lessons may be taught with subject areas. Drop everything for Peace is a PEF approach that sets aside time on a regular basis to teach only PEF components and curriculums.[89]

Mediation programs can help manage and resolve conflicts between young people, between young people and adults, and between adults. The principal, teachers, or other adults can be trained as mediators to help young people and adults resolve their disputes. Within these settings, mediation programs are established to reduce disciplinary actions, encourage effective problem solving, improve school or agency climate, and provide an alternative forum for problem solving.[90]

Youth mediators help resolve disputes between peers involving jealousies, rumors, misunderstandings, bullying, fights, personal property, and damaged friendships. Youth and adults may co-mediate

---

87　Safe Schools Program Director, Palm Beach County Schools. P. 18.
88　F. Schmidt, and A. Friedman, Fighting Families, Miami, FL: Peace 10 Education Foundation. 1994, 18.
89　Ibid., 19.
90　F. Schrumpf, D. Crawford, and R. Bodine, Peer Mediation: Conflict Resolution in Schools, Revised edition, Champaign, IL: Research Press, Inc. 1996, 23.

conflicts such as personality clashes, issues of respect and behavior, as other conflicts damage youth/adult relationships.[91]

During the mediation, the mediator uses the six problem-solving steps of conflict resolution. To set the stage by establishing ground rules for problem solving, identify interests contributing to the conflict, create options that address the interests of both disputants, gather perspectives by listening to each disputants paint of view, generate an agreement satisfactory to each disputant, and evaluate these options according to objective criteria.

Although the mediator controls the process, the disputants control the outcome. Participation in mediation is voluntary, and the mediatory does not judge, impose an agreement, or force a solution. Conflicts can only be resolved if the disputants choose to resolve them. Disputants are more likely to execute the terms of an agreement if they have authored them, because they can judge best what will resolve the conflict.

Table 2: Recommended Time for Peer Mediation Training

Grade Level	Minimum Number of Hours of Training
Elementary school	12-16
Middle school	12-16
High school	15-20[92]

Peer mediation programs are among the most widely chosen types of conflict resolution programs in school. Young people understand their peers, make the process age appropriate, empower their peers and command their respect, and normalize the conflict resolution process.

Young people can connect with their peers in ways that adults cannot. Young people perceive peer mediation as a way to talk out problems without the fear of an adult judging their behavior, thoughts, or feelings. When young people solve their own problems, they feel

---

91   Ibid.
92   National Association for Mediation in Education. 1995. Standards for Peer Mediation Programs, Washington, DC: National Institute for Dispute Resolution.

they are in control and can make commitments to the solutions they have created.

Disputes between two students are handled by a team of two student mediators, and disputes between a staff member and a student are handled by a student and staff mediator team. A peer mediation program must be perceived as fulfilling the needs of both faculty and students. A broad based coalition of administrators, classroom teachers, special educators, counselors, deans, social workers, and health educators interested in developing a conflict resolution program is necessary for a successful program. This team may also include students, parents, or community members. Because the members initiate the program and are charged with gaining the support of the entire school staff, the team is the key to a successful program.

The program team must be trained to become informed decision makers, effective implementers, and strong advocates for the program. Content for the training includes understanding conflict, principles of conflict resolution, social and cultural diversity and conflict resolution, mediation process and skills, program organization and operation, role of peer mediation in the school, and rationale for peer mediation.[93]

Figure 3: The Six Developmental Phases of the Mediation Program of the Illinois Institute for Dispute Resolution

Phase I:	**Develop the Program Team and Commitment** • Create program team. • Train program team. • Designate program coordinators. • Conduct needs assessment. • Build faculty consensus for program development.
Phase II:	**Design and Plan the Program** • Develop timeline for implementation. • Establish advisory committee. • Develop policies and procedures. • Identify and develop funding sources.

---

93   N. Copeland, and F. Garfield, Resolving Conflict: Activities for Grades K-3, Albuquerque, NM: Center for Dispute Resolutions, 1989.

Phase III:	**Select and Train the Mediators** • Conduct student orientation. • Select peer mediators. • Train mediators. • Recognize peer mediators.
Phase IV:	**Educate a Critical Mass** • Conduct faculty in service training. • Conduct student workshops. • Provide family and community orientation. • Offer parent workshops.
Phase V:	**Develop and Execute a Promotional Campaign** • Execute initial campaign. • Develop ongoing promotion.
Phase VI:	**Program Operation and Maintenance** • Request mediation process. • Schedule mediations and mediators. • Supervise mediation session. • Provide mediators ongoing training and support. • Evaluate prograrn.[94]

William Kreidler, a pioneer of the peaceable classroom, views the classroom as a caring and respectful community having five qualities: cooperation, communication, emotional expression, appreciation for diversity, and conflict resolution. Peaceable classrooms build the capacity of youth to manage and resolve conflict on their own by learning to recognize the role of perceptions and biases, identify feelings and factors that cause escalation, improve listening skills in order to handle anger and understand and analyze conflict, identify common interests, brainstorm multiple options that address interests, create a win-win agreement, evaluate the consequences of different options.

The faculty teaches students to be peacemakers by teaching understanding the nature of conflict. Learning includes recognizing conflicts by focusing attention on problems, increasing higher level

---

94   Bodine, Crawford, and Schrumpf, 28.

cognitive and moral reasoning, increasing motivation to learn, providing insights into other perspectives and life experiences.

The faculty teaches students to choose an appropriate conflict strategy. Two concerns when facing a conflict are achieving their goals and maintaining a good relationship with the other person. The balance between the two determines whether they should withdraw; giving up both the goals and the relationship; force achieving the goal at the other person's expense, thereby giving up the relationship; smooth, giving up the goal to enhance the relationship; compromise, giving up part of the goal at some damage to the relationship; or negotiate, solving the problem, thus achieving the goal and maintaining the relationship.

Participants are taught that in long-term relationships, the most important strategy is the problem solving process of negotiations, such as those with schoolmates and faculty. When negotiating to solve the problem, it is not enough to tell students to be nice or talk it out, or solve your problem. This training teaches students, faculty, and administrators specific procedures for negotiating disputants to meet their goals while improving the quality of their relationships.

By cooling before mediation begins, the mediation sets the ground rules and introduces the process of mediation. This helps the disputants successfully negotiate with each other. Formalize the agreement by completing a report form and having disputants sign it as a commitment to implement the agreement and abide by its conditions.

Figure 4: The Problem-Solving Negotiation Procedure

Describe what you want. *"I want to use the book now."* This involves using good communication skills and defining the conflict as a small and specific mutual problem.
Describe how you feel. *"I'm frustrated."* Disputants must understand how they feel and communicate it accurately and unambiguously.

Describe the reason for your wants and feelings. *"You have been using the book/or the past hour. If I don't get to use the book soon, my report will not be done on time. It's frustrating to have to wait so long."* This step includes expressing cooperative intentions, listening carefully, separating interests from positions, and differentiating before trying to integrate the two sets of interests.

Take the other's perspective and summarize your understanding of what the other person wants, how the other person feels, and the reasons underlying both. *"My understanding of you is ..."* This includes understanding the perspective of the opposing disputant and being able to see the problem from both perspectives simultaneously.

Invent three optional plans to resolve the conflict that maximize joint benefits. *"Plan A is ... Plan B is ... Plan C is ..."* These are creative optional agreements that maximize the benefits fro all disputants and solve the problem.

Choose the wisest course of action and formalize the agreement with a handshake. *"Let's agree on Plan B!"* A wise agreement is fair to all disputants, maximizes joint benefits, and strengthens disputants' ability to work together cooperatively and resolve future conflicts constructively. It specifies how each disputant should act and how the agreement will be reviewed and renegotiated if it does not work.[95]

The peaceable school approach integrates conflict resolution into the operation of the school. Peaceable school climates reflect caring, honesty, cooperation, and appreciation for diversity. Every member of the school community learns and uses conflict resolution concepts and skills:

- Cooperative learning environments;
- Direct instruction and practice of conflict resolution skills and processes;
- Non-coercive school and classroom management systems;
- Integration of conflict resolution concepts and skills into the curriculum.

95   D.W. Johnson, and R.T. Johnson, Teaching Students To Be Peacemakers, Edina, MN: Interaction Book Company, 1991, 3:52-3:60.

Peaceable school programs challenge youth and adults to believe that a diverse society and nonviolent society is a realistic and desirable goal. It is encouraged in peaceable schools to promote peacemaking as the normative behavior of adults and students. All participants in a peaceable school apply conflict resolution skills addressing problems and issues that confront students, faculty, administrators, and parents. The main objectives of peacemaking are to achieve personal, group, and institutional goals and to maintain cooperative relationships.

The classroom is the unit block where students gain this knowledge and skill needed to resolve conflicts creatively with the majority of conflicts addressed.[96] Peer mediation is applied as a service in the classroom to help disputing students settle their differences. To gain effectual conflict resolution behavior, participants are required to develop mutual appreciation and respect. The goal of the peaceable school is to create a school-wide discipline program focused on empowering students to regulate and control their own behavior. Through cooperation and persistent pursuit of constructive behavior, the program allows educators to model an orderly, productive system. Conflict resolution enables students to achieve principled responses with problem-solving processes. The behavior management program becomes an educational program. Students are provided ways to behave, and not just told to refrain from behaving in a certain manner.

The training for professional development for teachers and staff presents the theory and methods of conflict resolution, intercultural understanding, and emotional and social literacy. It prepares teachers and staff to model and teach these skills in their classrooms, illustrating ways to incorporate conflict resolution strategies and skills into academic subjects, creative teaching techniques such as role-playing, interviewing, brainstorming, small group sharing, and cooperative learning teams.

Teachers can plan classroom activities and find resources, see skilled practitioners give demonstration lessons in the classroom with the staff development component. This also gives the teachers opportunity to receive feedback on lessons that they teach.

---

96   D, Johnson, and R. Johnson, "Cooperative Learning and Conflict Resolution," The Fourth R 42:8, 1993, 39.

The Resolving Conflict Creatively Program (RCCP) is initives of Educators for Social Responsibility (ESR). The ESR model provides a theoretical background on key topics social and emotional learning and developmentally appropriate classroom teaching activities. The RCCP, adults reach young people by relating to them daily in their homes, schools, and communities.; requiring the support of the highest levels of the school's administration before the program is implemented. It has to have a participating school district to make its vision for change and commitment to multi-year involvement to ensure proper operation of the program. The RCCP involves: professional development for teachers and other staff, classroom instruction based on a kindergarten through 12th grade (K-12) curriculum, peer mediation, administrator training, as well as parent training.[97]

Table 3: Punishment Versus Discipline

Punishment	Discipline
Expresses power of an authority; causes pain to the recipient; based on retribution or revenge; concerned with actions in the past.	Based on logical or natural consequences that embody the reality of a social order (rules that one must learn and accept to function productively in society); concerned with actions in the present.
Arbitrary-probably applied inconsistently and unconditionally; does not accept or acknowledge exceptions or mitigating circumstances.	Consistent; accepts that the behaving individual is doing the best he or she can do for now.
Imposed by an authority with responsibility assumed by the one administering the punishment and responsibility avoided by the one receiving the punishment.	Comes from within, with responsibility assumed by the disciplined individual who desires that responsibility; presumes that conscience is internal.

---

97   G. Konopka, "A Renewed Look at Human Development, Human Needs, and Human Services," Proceedings of the Annual Gisela Konopka Lectureship. St. Paul, MN: University of Minnesota Center for Youth Development and Research, 1985, 186.

Closes options for the punished individual, who must pay for a behavior that has already occurred.	Opens options for the individual, who can choose new behavior.
As a teaching strategy, usually reinforces a failure identity. Essentially negative and short-term, without sustained personal involvement of either teacher or learner.	As a teaching strategy, is active and involves close, sustained, personal involvement of both teacher and learner; emphasizes the development of more successful behavior.
Characterized by open or concealed anger; easy and expedient; a poor model of expectations.	Friendly and supportive; provides a model of quality behavior.
Focuses on strategies intended to control behavior of learner; rarely results in positive changes in behavior; may increase subversiveness or result in temporary suppression of behavior; at best, produces compliance.	Usually results in a change in behavior that is more successful, acceptable, and responsible; develops the capacity for self-evaluation of behavior.[98]

Administration training introduces the concepts of conflict resolution and bias awareness. It encourages administrators to model the same human and creative approaches to dealing with conflict that teachers are providing through the classroom curriculum.

There is a 12 hour training in the skills for parents to participate in, with inter group relations, so they can make their homes more peaceful, which will help their children become adept at using the skills learned at school. As parents learn more ways of dealing with conflict and prejudice at home, they are able to be better leaders in the schools and communities. After participating in a district-level 60 hour training program, parents may become trainers of other parents. Parents attend workshops that teach skills and concepts of conflict

98   D. Crawford, R. Bodine, and R. Hoglund, The School for Quality Learning. Champaign, IL: Research Press, Inc., 1993, 187.

resolution. They learn to apply these concepts with their families in their homes, schools, and communities.

Peer education is a must for school youth. They are recruited to form a Youth Peace Corps trained to teach conflict resolution strategies, including anger management. These youths provide strong role models for younger students because they teach these skills in the school and use their skills in the neighborhood.

Community training may be provided for youth serving organizations and those who encounter youth in conflict; such as police departments, park districts, Boys and Girls Clubs, the Urban League, and other interested agencies and organizations that work with youth. Specific personnel from the different community agencies are recruited for the training.

After school sessions and Saturdays can bring community members together to learn about one another and practice conflict resolution skills. Activities lead to the team demonstrating how to solve problems together. This allows the participants to confront their differences as well as their interdependency.[99]

Peacemaking is not easy. In many ways, it is much more difficult than making war; but, its great rewards cannot be measured in ordinary terms.[100]

Implementing conflict resolution for juvenile justice facilities and alternative schools means changing the punitive system to one that uses problem solving methods. However, in these settings, the program only supplements and does not replace existing disciplinary policies and procedures. Youth learn, given the opportunities for positive expression and problem resolution, through alternatives to violent and self-defeating behavior. The program must address the psychological needs and the developmental stage of the youth. These programs do not offer therapy. Youths who need therapy can still participate in the program by getting their therapy from the appropriate services.

---

99   Konopka, 186.
100   J. Carter, Talking Peace: A Vision for the Next Generation, New York, NY: Dutton Children's Books, 1993, p. xiv.

Many juvenile offenders have deficits in cooperative skills. They tend to lack the values, attitudes, reasoning abilities and social skills required for positive social interaction.

The juvenile justice correctional facility provides opportunities over alternative education settings, because the students live and attend school within the facility. This can allow more time for training and to practice conflict resolution.[101]

In 1987, with support from California's office of Criminal Justice Planning, the Community Board Program began to explore how the conflict manager (peer mediation) program might be implemented in juvenile treatment facilities known as ranches. In some states, these facilities are the last chance for the rehabilitation of serious and violent juvenile offenders before they enter the youth authority, the juvenile equivalent of the adult prison system.

The conflict manager program helps everyone involved deal with conflict more effectively. Over time, unresolved conflicts can affect the entire facility, maldng the atmosphere tense and anxious, lowering the morale of counselors and wards, by consuming the time and energy of everyone.

Superintendent Harold Holden, of the Ranch for Boys, states,

> Our boys are here in part because they have experienced conflict in their lives and did not know how to resolve it appropriately. The conflict manager program teaches these young men the skills to approach a conflict in a mature manner and resolve it in a socially acceptable fashion.[102]

The conflict manager program is a face-to-face session with the disputants to talk about their problems with the conflict managers who are the mediators for their peers.

---

101 M. Holmberg, and J. Halligan, Conflict Management for Juvenile Treatment Facilities: A Manual for Training and Program Implementation, San Francisco, CA: Community Board Program, Inc., 1992, 47.

102 G.M. Sadalla, and M. Holmberg, Conflict Resolution: A Secondary Curriculum, San Francisco, CA: Community Board Program, Inc., 1987, 48.

The disputants, throughout, are required to take full responsibility for the problem and its solution. The conflict managers help the disputants understand one another's point of view. To rebuild or establish a positive relationship between the disputants and spread the belief and use of peaceful and constructive conflict resolution skills throughout the facility, is the main objectives of conflict management.[103] Name calling, serious horseplay, and conflicts over things in short supply, such as time at the pool table, weight room, a chance to watch a television program, the attention of a popular counselor, or access to supplies such as toiletries-conflict managers are equipped to handle many of these day-to-day disputes existing in a juvenile facility setting. Violent confrontation, when weapons are involved, is a type of conflict that is not handled by conflict managers. After the battle has passed, this may go the managers to find ways to avoid further violence.

Because conflict management is voluntary, it is never a replacement for disciplinary action. The goal is to provide early intervention for peaceful problem solving before rules are broken or conflicts escalate. However, when wards break the rules, staff can take the usual disciplinary steps. Afterward, they can suggest meeting with conflict managers, hoping to resolve core issues and avoid any further conflict. Conflict manager programs only supplement and never replace the regular disciplinary system.

---

103   Ibid.

CONFLICT MANAGER TRAINING

Included in the training of conflict managers are: basic communication skills, questions to ask, and methods of handling common problems, as well as talking and listing in a way that will defuse anger, and speaking to disputants in a direct but diplomatic way.

Because of ward turnover, this training for new conflict managers is conducted every few months. Ongoing meeting among conflict managers are held to provide further training, assessment of the program, and group discussion.[104]

Another target for conflict is the alternative school. Students in most alternative schools do not differ from any other school when it comes to conflict. Therefore, they need not be treated differently when developing and implementing a conflict resolution program. Many of these youths are involved, or have been involved, in the court system and may be in an alternative school due to court dictates. Although many of these students are intellectually capable, they have often failed academically. Some are teen parents; some are homeless; others are involved in substance abuse. Most of these students have demonstrated, in one or many ways, that their behavior is unacceptable in a regular school. Most students in this situation need conflict resolution education because they have experienced numerous conflicts involving other youth, school staff members, and school expectations or rules. After they are in alternative schools because they escalated rather than de-escalated a dispute, these students are prime candidates for conflict resolution education.

In 1971, an alternative high school was established as part of a network in New York City. It had approximately 180 students and 14 teachers, including a site coordinator, at each of its four campuses. Students who have dropped out or at risk of dropping out, may apply voluntarily, while others are referred by school staff or the court system. The students have poor attendance records and a broad range of academic skills. The racial composition was 56.9% African

---

104 D. Prothrow-Stith, Violence Prevention: Curriculum for Adolescents, Newton, MA: Education Development Center, 1987, 49.

American, 40.5% Hispanic, 2.2% white, 0.4% Asian, and 0.1% Native American; 5.1% of the students had limited proficiency in English. The average age was 17 years with an equal number of female and male students. Many of the students came from disadvantaged households, with a large number from families with risk factors such as drug abuse and homelessness. Achievement rate was below other New York City high schools. The average that acquired credits were 20, and dropouts had been out of school for periods of six months to seven years.

The International Center for Corporation and Conflict Resolution training has the Deutsch's theoretical model, which offers a number of basic principles of conflict resolution, Raider's training model, Prothrow-Smith's curriculum on violence prevention and the Community Board Program's curriculum. All training is taught in a variety of ways. Sessions for new students, family groups, or vocational classes, done by role playing, group activities, and discussion groups are used to apply negotiation skills to the students in school, home and even work settings. The International Center for Corporation and Conflict Resolution reported that as their relations with others improved, these youths increased their self-esteem and decreased feelings of anxiety and depression, with more positive feelings of well-being. Greater self-esteem produced led to a much higher academic performance. These positive results suggest that cooperative learning and conflict resolution training are valuable in a wide range of settings.

PARENT AND COMMUNITY
INITIATIVES

This linkage is important because young people face a challenge in applying conflict resolution training in the community, in the home, and with others who are not similarly trained. Children must acquire skills that enable them to live in harmony with their families and the larger community. Development of these skills depends upon trusting and loving relationships, the first and most fundamental of which is between children and their parents. Families are the basic training ground for developing the capacity to function responsibly and to solve problems peacefully. Families are the settings where children's basic needs are met and where they learn lessons about personal relationships and problem solving. Children must possess a secure and positive sense of their own identity and their place in the world.

The circle is a sacred symbol of life. Individual parts within the circle connect with every other; and what happens to one, or what one part does, affects all within the circle.[105]

Interventions that affect the lives of young children are strengthening parenting bonds and teaching children self-discipline, and also conflict resolution. Children are less prone to violence when their basic needs are met and they are reared in consistent, safe, and loving environments. Early intervention is important to recognize that some youths are at risk for violence and should be provided with effective, comprehensive experiences in school, at home, and in the community. Beginning in elementary school, all children should be given "basic training" in self-discipline. Teachers can be trained to use naturally occurring discipline problems to create school cultures of nonviolence.

---

105 V.D.H. Sneve, "Women of the Circle," A Common Land, A Diverse People, H. Thompson, A. Huseboe, and S. Looney (eds.), Sioux Falls, SD: Nordland Heritage Foundation, 1987, 53.

Students need to be competent in resolving both conflicts with peers and authority problems with adults. This competence forms the basis for lifelong survival skills.

Table 4: Characteristics of Resilient Children

Social Competence	Problem-Solving	Sense of Autonomy
• Responsiveness to others. • Conceptual and intellectual flexibility • Caring for others • Good communication skills • Sense of humor.	• Ability to apply abstract training • Ability to engage in reflective thought • Critical reasoning skills • Ability to develop alternative solutions in frustrating situations.	• Positive sense of independence • Emerging feelings of efficacy • High self-esteem • Impulse control • Planning and goal setting • Belief in the future. [106]

In mentoring at-risk youth, it is a fact that every child needs at least one adult who provides unconditional love. Many children suffer greatly from attention deprivation when there are no parenting bonds. When parents are unable or unavailable to provide the consistent nurturing and support that children need, mentors can have a profound impact in fulfilling that role. There is a need for mentoring and training parents, also. Since much early antisocial behavior is caused by inconsistent and harsh discipline, parent training curriculums are important tools for breaking cycles of coercion (abuse and/or violence), and instilling positive parent-child interactions. By targeting bullies, we find that peer harassment is an early indicator of lifelong antisocial problems. Without intervention, childhood bullies often develop into violent adults.

When parents model effective behaviors in conflict situations, they present powerful teaching examples to children. Educating

---

106 B. Benard, "Fostering Resiliency in Kids," Educational Leadership. Reprinted with permission of the Association for Supervision and Curriculum Development, (November) 1993, 44-48.

parents in conflict resolution is a natural way to bring children's experiences at home and at school closer together. Helping families deal constructively with the inevitable conflicts of family living allows parents to disengage from inconsistent and harsh, punitive behaviors.

Many early childhood education programs include parent involvement and parent education components for intervening in behaviors that promote a cycle of violence. Parents are children's first and most influential teachers. The Parents as Teachers program, which originated in St. Louis, Missouri, is based on the idea that early childhood experiences are critical in laying the foundation for success in school and life.

Parents Anonymous, Inc., by recognizing the link between child abuse and juvenile delinquency, the office of Juvenile Justice and Delinquency Prevention (OJJDP) began to support Parents Anonymous, Inc. (PA) in 1994. Because minority children are over represented in the juvenile justice system, this collaborative effort between OJJDP and PA focuses on bringing PA' s comprehensive model of neighborhood based, shared leadership to families in low income, high crime areas. This is implemented in 11 states by PA to serve the ethnic groups, including Native Americans, African Americans, Asians, Latinos, and Applachiens.

Two other agencies joined to create a project providing comprehensive direct services in the form of mediation, parent and staff mediation training, and bias awareness training are Franklin Mediation Services and Head Start of Franklin County, Massachusetts. Advocates who regularly work with Head Start families report that the concepts and skills learned in the program become part of family conflict management.

Both community-to-school and school-to-community programs also make critical linkages that will enhance the quality of life in each arena. By providing youths with conflict resolution training through churches, youth clubs, courts, other referral services, and other organizations, lessons learned through follow up training at school are reinforced.

Mediation centers are located in more than 600 communities in the United States. These centers have initiated the community-to-school link in developing and implementing conflict resolution programs for children, youth, and families. Using trained volunteers to provide a wide range of mediation services to youth and adults, these centers are typically nonprofit community based agencies. The centers have collaborated with other youth serving agencies and schools in the development of prevention and intervention strategies and initiatives to prevent youth violence. The mediation centers have pioneered applications of mediation for youth and families, including truancy, parent/child, gang, and suspension mediation, as well as in juvenile correctional settings. To prevent youth violence, centers have collaborated with other youth serving agencies and schools in the development of prevention and intervention strategies.

Figure 5: C.H.O.I.C.E.S. for Managing Conflict

• **Commands:** Give clear directions and specifically state what you want the child to do in a non-humiliating manner-"Clean up your room before visiting your friend."
• **Humor or surprise:** Use non-sarcastic humor or do the unexpected to defuse an explosive situation. For example, channel kids who are bickering over a toy into a different activity-"Let's pretend we're robots and clean up the family room."
• **Offer choices:** Give a choice between two options-"You can _____ or _____," or "When you _____, then you can _____"
• **Ignore:** Choose not to address the conflict or unacceptable behavior by withholding attention.
• **Compromise:** Seek a middle ground by finding a solution that partially satisfies both parties-"If you _____, then I'll _____ "
• **Encourage problem solving:** Work together to explore the disagreement, generate alternatives, and find a solution that satisfies the needs of both parties-"What can we do to meet everyone's needs?"
• **Structure the environment:** Rearrange people, room structure, or objects to reduce conflict. For example, separate kids who are fighting in the car by moving them to different seats.[107]

107 S. Beekman, and J. Holmes, Battles, Hassles, Tantrums & Tears: Strategies for Coping with Conflict and Making Peace at Home, New York, NY: Hearst Books, William Morrow & Company, Inc., Publishers, 1993, 90.

In recruitment and selection of community youth, networking is perhaps the most important key to developing a community based program. Youths were recruited from other organizations, such as Boys and Girls Clubs, church programs, court referral programs, and other self-esteem programs for youth in the area. The community outreach goals are aimed at spreading conflict resolution. Community outreach can reach youths that are not in school, clubs and other programs, by developing a high-school-age conflict resolution and negotiation curriculum, training teachers, youth, and community members to teach the curriculum, and designing a model program (including training and curriculum) for replication in other communities.

Conflict resolution training must be comprehensive to be effective in changing the way young people respond to conflict. Reinforcement of community based programs is needed to help young people see what conflict resolution measures can be implemented at home and on the street, as well as at school. A community based program can resolve any conflict youth might have about mixed messages about how to deal proactively with conflict. Example: If youth learn problem solving processes in the school environment and a competitive winner-take-all approach at home or on the street, they will resort to the method that is reinforced and addresses their needs for safety and security.

Parents can perform some functions with limited training, but certain duties, such as training conflict managers and facilitating biweekly meetings, require intensive training. Parents are encouraged to become involved in a variety of ways. They can perform some functions with limited training. Parents may join teachers in a two-day mediation training, or attend a series of workshops introducing them to effective family communication and problem solving skills for use in the home. Parent support groups meet in the schools to discuss concerns and participate in ongoing skills training and practice. A well informed parent group also serves as an important referral source. They can present information at parent-teacher association meetings, student and/or parent assemblies, staff meetings, town meetings, and students' classes.

Youth as young as age 14 are trained to become community mediators. Students provide important additional resources for the community mediator program. The youth also learn valuable resources about citizenry, as well as conflict resolution skills.

Cross-referral system, if a school has no peer mediation program, educators can benefit from understanding the sorts of disputes that might be referred to community mediation programs.

COMMUNITY BUY-IN AND IMPLICATIONS FOR REPLICATION

Some helpful steps to take in building programs are conducting a needs assessment for conflict resolution training in the community, developing a program that builds on existing programs and fills gaps in conflict resolution training, and creating and implementing a fund-raising plan.

The community board programs, throughout the United States, have been at the forefront of bring conflict resolution services and programming to schools, families, and other youth settings. Because youth spend time in both schools and communities, strong connections between the two can benefit them in many ways. Young people in need of neighborhood based services receive more effective referrals when schools and communities are more aware of each other.[108]

Through a grant from the Bureau of Justice Assistance, Office of Justice Programs, U.S. Department of Justice, the Boys and Girls Clubs of America has developed a violence prevention program that includes the Second Step foundation skills curriculum developed by the Committee for Children. The program teaches club members the problem solving processes of conflict resolution, anger management, impulse control, and empathy. Also, the Boys and Girls Clubs provide information and training on mediation.

---

108   Beekman, and Holmes, 59.

These programs have assisted our members in reducing the level of interpersonal violence and in supporting a positive peaceful environment in their respective communities. We look forward to their important message reaching all our youth members in all our Boys and Girls Clubs.[109]

Conflicts arise when parents feel that their children's race or ethnicity is not being treated sensitively by teachers, counselors, and administrators. Conflicts also arise in schools when different student groups stalce out turf in certain areas of the school, i.e., the cafeteria, the resource room, or the athletic fields, or during school dances and sports events. When racist graffiti appears in the restroom or other parts of the campus, and when they form gangs on campus.

Some clues for recognizing the warning signs of tension building up in the community and school are what racial and ethnic groups attend the school, where they live in relation to one another, and how these groups get to and from school. Do activities in the school bring together diverse groups? What has been the history of interaction among these various groups?

Urban Smarts is a 14 week program. Each school is assigned a team of three professional artists, four caseworkers, several volunteers, and one teacher/counselor. Program goals include improving social behavior and skills through the arts, developing art skills and providing opportunities for performance and exhibitions, and diverting at risk youth from the juvenile justice system through the arts and conflict resolution education.

Developed by the Learning Systems Group, the Department of Education's Safe and Dmg-Free Schools program funded the development of several arts and prevention projects. These projects have incorporated many building blocks that have strengthened young people's ability to work together and to learn as well as practice conflict resolution.

Using the arts to teach the message that conflicts can be resolved without violence is exciting and offers many opportunities to bring teachers, parents, and other members of the community into the

---

109 J.D. Cox, Personal Cormnunication, (May) 1996.

process potential for addressing social problems through the arts. Teams working together bring results of completed art projects through peaceful conflict resolution. Students learned not only the process of an art form, but also nonviolent alternatives to conflicts. Research in this field indicates that conflict resolution and mediation programs show positive effects in reducing violence.

Early research, in 1974, DeCecco and Richards published the results of one of the most comprehensive studies on conflict within schools. They interviewed more than 8,000 students and 500 faculty members in more than 60 junior and senior high schools in New York City, Philadelphia, and San Francisco. They found that more than 90% of the conflicts reported by students were unresolved or resolved in destructive ways-negotiation practically nonexistent. Conflict resolution programs conducted in 17 schools between 1990 and 1993, improved student attitudes toward conflict, increased understanding of nonviolent problem solving methods, and enhanced communication skills.

Figure 6: Risk Factors for Health and Behavior Problems

Adolescent Problems Behaviors [110]					
Risk Factor	Substance Abuse	Delinquency	Teenage Pregnancy	School Dropout	Violence
Community					
Availability of drugs	✓				
Availability of firearms		✓			✓
Community laws and norms favorable toward drug use, firearms, and crime	✓	✓			✓
Media portrayals of violence					✓
Transitions and mobility	✓	✓		✓	
Low neighborhood attachment and community organization	✓	✓			✓
Extreme economic deprivation	✓	✓	✓	✓	✓
Family					
Family history of the problem behavior	✓	✓	✓	✓	
Family management problems	✓	✓	✓	✓	✓
Family conflict	✓	✓	✓	✓	✓
Favorable parental attitudes and involvement in the problem behavior	✓	✓			✓
School					
Early and persistent antisocial behavior	✓	✓	✓	✓	✓
Academic failure beginning in elementary school	✓	✓	✓	✓	✓
Lack of commitment to school	✓	✓	✓	✓	
Individual/Peer					
Rebelliousness	✓	✓		✓	
Friends who engage in the problem behavior	✓	✓	✓	✓	✓
Favorable attitudes toward the problem behavior	✓	✓	✓	✓	
Early initiation of the problem behavior	✓	✓	✓	✓	✓
Constitutional factors	✓	✓			✓

---

110   Catalano, R., and J.D. Hawkins, Communities That Care, 1995, 10.

AGE-APPROPRIATE SEQUENCE FOR ACQUIRING FOUNDATION ABILITIES OF CONFLICT RESOLUTION

Sufficient and diverse age-appropriate activities that give students the opportunity for practice, evaluation, and further practice are crucial to the success of any conflict resolution program. From early childhood to grade two, the student is able to understand that conflict is natural and involvement in conflict is okay. He/she has learned that conflicts can be solved through cooperation, views peace as a desired condition, and differentiates between prejudice and dislike. The student's perception ability accepts that he/she is not always right. At that age, he/she can describe conflict from his/her own perspective and from the perspective of others. Emotionally, the student controls anger, knowing that feeling anger, frustration and fear is all right. Through creative thinking ability, he student expresses feelings and acknowledges the feelings of others. He/she describes what is desired and why, and generates ideas for solving a problem. Communication abilities enable the student to listen, describe an incident, ask and answer questions. Through critical thinking abilities, the student chooses from multiple ideas, understands fairness to self and to another person, expresses plans for resolving a conflict, and understands the meaning of committing to a plan and being trustworthy.

From grades three to five, students have learned that conflict is inevitable and can become better or worse, depending on the chosen response. The students recognize prejudice in self and in the actions of others, understands his/her own behavior in terms of the need for belonging, power, freedom, and fun. Perception abilities identify and check own assumptions about a situation and understand how others perceive words and actions, empathizing and accepting the feelings and perception of others. At this level students understand friendships and strive to build and maintain them. He/she understands both his own emotions and that the emotional responses of others may be different from his/her own. The students are able to express emotions effectively and appropriately without being disagreeable. Creative thinking abilities allow students to distinguish and identify interests and positions, both mutual and compatible and create behavioral options to satisfy those interests. Through communication abilities, the students summarize facts and feelings, recognizing nonverbal communication by self and by others. His/her critical thinking abilities allow realistic evaluation of the risks and consequences of "flight or fight" in conflict and identify the best self-help alternative in a situation. By evaluating interests of self and others according to fairness standards, students craft win-win resolutions.

From grades six to eight, the students' orientation abilities allow them to recognize that the sources of conflict and the problem solving processes of conflict resolution are applicable to all types of conflicts-interpersonal, intergroup, and international. They are able to diagnose conflicts appropriately and select conflict resolution strategies for conflicts in various settings, i.e., school, home, and neighborhood. The students recognize the limitations of their own perceptions and understand selective filters affect seeing and hearing. At this point, perception abilities recognize the prevalence and glamorization of violence in society, and that conflicts can escalate into violence. These students takes responsibility for their emotions, while accepting and validating emotions and perceptions of others. He/she possess effective strategies for "cool down" and use them at appropriate times. Creative thinking abilities allow students to understand that underlying interests, not positions, define the problem in conflict situations and that multiple, unclear, or conflicting interests often coexist. The students use analytical tools to diagnose and problem solve for conflicting as well as compatible interests. Using summarizing and clarifying to defuse anger and de-escalate conflict, the student is productively persuasive. He/she listens to understand, and speak, to be understood, reframing his/her own statements using unbiased and less inflammatory language. Using critical thinking abilities, these students challenge assumptions about what is possible, consider short-and-long-term consequences of proposed options. They negotiate without conceding, recognizing the efficacy of committing only to solutions that are fair, realistic, and workable.

From grades nine to twelve, the student maintain good working relationships with parents, family, siblings, boyfriends, girlfriends, teachers, and bosses by analyzing conflict in the context of a present relationship and using an appropriate problem solving strategy. He/she understands that conflict resolution skills are life skills, and recognizes patterns in his/her responses to conflict and strives for positive growth and change in those patterns. He/she confronts prejudice effectively in self and others and seeks diverse and multi cultural experiences and relationships, actively working to promote peace in the school and in the community. The student critically analyzes his/her own perceptions and modifies his/her understanding as new information emerges. Understanding how problem solving strategies can be influenced, the student chooses to exercise positive influence and prevent escalation of conflicts, even with adults. Thus, he/she helps others recognize the potential for violence and for nonviolent resolution. Emotionally, the student remains calm and focused on problem solving when confronted by a strong emotional display from another person, including an adult. He/she evaluates and reconciles positions and interests of self and others in most situations. By prioritizing interests and developing a strategy for working toward agreement, the student articulates mutual interests and reconciles conflicting interests, brainstorms effectively, improving, refining, and expanding on current options. Using analytical tools to diagnose problems, he/she develops and evaluates new approaches. His/her communication abilities enable the student to summarize positions and interests of others in conflict situations efficiently and accurately. He/she acknowledges the validity of emotions and perspectives of others, using clarifying questions to uncover hidden interests of others. The student speculates as to best alternatives to a negotiated agreement for self and others, analyzing ways to improve the best alternatives. He/she uses problem solving processes when engaging in difficult conversations and identifies uncontrollable factors that might impact the ability of the parties to fulfill an agreement. Identifying external standards of fairness and using those to resolve conflicts, the student honors commitments and encourages others to do the same.

Table 5: Age-Appropriate Sequence for Acquiring the Problem-solving Processes of Conflict Resolution

Early Childhood to Grade 2	Grades 3-5	Grades 6-9	Grades 9-12
Negotiation Process			
• Cooperates with a peer in unassisted problem solving--each cools off, tells what happened, imagines ways to problem solve, and chooses a solution. • Participates in a negotiation session coached by an adult or older child.	• Manages the negotiation process without assistance.	• Performs principled negotiation with peers and adults. • Involves a peer who has little or no conflict resolution training in the negotiation process. • Understands that nearly every inter- action is a negotiation. • Teaches younger students the negotiation process.	• Negotiates with difficult parties effectively. • Teaches negotiation process to peers and adults. • Enjoys negotiation process.
Mediation Process			
• Participates in a mediation facilitated by an adult or older student mediator.	• Participates in the mediation process facilitated by another student or an adult. • Serves as a peer mediator in a class- room program or a school-wide program..	• Mediates disputes among peers. • Co-mediates disputes between peers and adults. • Coaches younger students and peers as they learn to mediate.	• Mediates an array of disputes involving various disputants. • Trains others in the mediation process.

Consensus Decision making Process			
• Engages in group problem solving discussions and processes facilitated by a teacher or other adult.	• Participates in class-room sessions designed to resolve group conflicts and problems.	• Manages consensus problem solving sessions for class-room groups of younger students. • Manages consensus decision making in a small group of peers (such as classroom work group or student council committee).	• Manages consensus problem solving in various groups. • Facilitates consensus decision making as a member of a group.

A needs assessment is critical to establishing a conflict resolution education program that moves beyond the efforts of individual staff toward a united effort to the entire school community. Some questions to consider for assessing the needs are:

1. To what extent are conflicts interfering with teaching and learning processes within the school?

2. What percentage of conflicts is attributable to:
   a. The competitive atmosphere of the school or classroom?
   b. An intolerant atmosphere in the school or classroom?
   c. Poor communication?
   d. Inappropriate expression of emotion?
   e. Lack of conflict resolution skills?
   f. Adult misuse of authority in the school or classroom?

3. To what extent are diversity issues manifested as conflicts in the school community?

4. To what extent is representation in decision making an issue manifested in the conflicts observed in the school?

5. What percentage of the conflicts arising in the school is:
   a. Between students?
   b. Between teachers and students?
   c. Between teachers?
   d. Between students and school expectations, rules, or policies?
   e. Between teachers and administrators?
   f. Between school staff and parents?
   g. Between other groups specific to the school?

6. What procedures are followed when conflicts cause disruption of teaching and learning processes? Who administers which procedures?

7. Who are the sources of referrals to these procedures?

8. How effective are these procedures according to the perceptions of students? parents? teachers? administrators? others?

9. What existing attitudes or behavior will facilitate the implementation of a conflict resolution program in the school? Who exhibits these?

10. What existing attitudes or behavior will impede the implementation of a conflict resolution program in the school? Who exhibits these?

11. Which foundation skills for conflict resolution are now included in the school curriculum? When are they developed? Who provides the training in these skills? Which students receive this training?

12. Which staff members have training in conflict resolution? How many hours of training?

13. Which staff development opportunities in conflict resolution are available? What opportunities are desired?

14. What present and future monetary resources are available to support implementation of a conflict resolution program?

15. What conflict resolution processes currently exist within the school? Within the school community?

16. What community resources exist to assist the school in designing and implementing a conflict resolution program?[111]

Important Factors for Successful Implementation

Universal success factors for conflict resolution education programs are the commitment and support of the administration, faculty, and parents. Research findings and practitioner experience support the idea that tailoring a program to a given site strengthens the probability of its success.

Administrators provide leadership and support for programs in a variety of ways. Leadership and support from both the school's and the school district's administration make for a successful conflict resolution education. Using staff meetings and parent meetings to discuss programs and their benefits in relations to student/adult outcomes, participation in training and staff development programs, and leading staff meetings and problem solving sessions using conflict resolution processes provides very good support. Program success recognition during assemblies, school-wide announcements, parent teacher association meetings, school board meetings and on other occasions gives an added boost. Making use of effective conflict management and the language of conflict resolution in the school and

---

[111] Bodine, Crawford, & Schrumpf, 53.

on the playground, and teaching or co-teaching conflict resolution lessons in the classrooms provides further support and leadership.

Faculty/Parent Commitment and Support

Without adequate planning and training, a program is unlikely sustainable. When you have a shared vision among faculty, you have a building block of program success. One way to gain faculty commitment is to involve them in program development through a strategic planning process.

Parent support is important to the success of programs and can be built through presentations at parent meetings in the school and in the community. Parents, like administrators and faculty, need to understand the programs that are being implemented in their children's school. Parents can also serve as volunteers helping to implement the program, or can attend conflict resolution training designed especially for them. Involving parents extends conflict resolution beyond the classroom.

PROGRAM EVALUATION

It is very important to remember that conflict resolution education is not a quick fix. The impact of conflict resolution programs occurs over time. Implementing a conflict resolution program is an extremely complex process that demands considerable energy and time from the adults involved.

An evaluation must show whether the program is reaching its goals (student and adult outcomes) and how it is enhancing the learning process. Any program in schools today needs to establish performance goals and to measure progress toward achieving those goals.[112]

---

112 J. Reno, "Attorney General Announces New Effort to Prevent School Violence," U.S. Department of Justice press release, May 29, 1996, 88.

Strategic planning is crucial in processing the formulation of a plan for bringing conflict resolution education into the school setting. A team works on a plan developing a conflict resolution program by collaborating with the entire school faculty. The plan is based on the results of the needs assessment.

The belief statements are the basis for obtaining the school's commitment to a specific mission to implement a program:

- Conflict is a natural part of everyday life.
- Conflict is an opportunity to grow and learn.
- Neither avoidance nor violence are healthy responses to conflict.
- Through awareness of cultural differences, we grow to respect others and to cherish diversity.
- Adults provide powerful behavior models for students; this is especially true in dealing with conflict.
- Students can learn to resolve some of their conflicts without adult involvement.

The mission of the conflict resolution education program is to teach students and faculty to resolve conflicts productively, to promote mutual understanding of individuals and groups throughout the school, and to enhance the climate of the school. The mission is the cornerstone upon which the entire plan for the program is built. The mission statement is the primary focus of the program.

Goals are the map for achieving the mission and give direction to all implementation planning. Goals are expressions of the desired outcomes of the conflict resolution program for students and adults in the school. Goals guide the setting of priorities and will provide the framework for evaluation of the program. Examples of goals for a program are:

- Students will utilize the conflict resolution processes of negotiation, mediation, and consensus decision making to resolve problems between students, between students and adults, and among groups.

- Adults will utilize the conflict resolution processes of negotiation, mediation, and consensus decision making to resolve problems between students, between students and adults, and among groups.

The action plan delineates the tasks required to select and implement a conflict resolution program. Development of an action plan is an ongoing process. As tasks are completed, new ones are given. Important factors for successful implementation are programs designed to address specific concerns, using existing resources, and build the capacity of staff are more likely to sustain.

There are pitfalls to avoid; never begin to implement a programs without proper preparation. Careful planning and training will lead to a better, more successful program.

Administration and faculty who feel no responsibility for achieving the program's goals will not help support the program. Failure to match the program and trainers to the school's needs will result in major problems for the program. Selecting the trainer who is not qualified or who will not build the school's training capacity will create future problems for the program.

chapter four

NEW APPROACHES TO RESOLVING CONFLICT

WORKPLACE DISPUTES

Anyone involved in work recognizes that conflict is a part of it. As interaction takes place on the job, people seek to accomplish individual and organizational objectives, and workers carry out a variety of workplace roles; conflict comes with this territory, and at times, it gets out of hand. However, it is important to note that some conflict in the workplace is beneficial, even necessary.[113]

Staff who is in unanimous agreement with his/her managements every idea may result in harmony, but it will not result in the best ideas and approaches to solving problems. Conflict that results from the expression of differing viewpoints, innovative proposals, and diverse expressions will often yield for better results. With this kind of conflict, you will have growth and serve the organization well.[114]

On the other hand, conflict can also be highly destructive to the organization and the people in it. This kind of conflict often results from communication failures, personality clashes, differing values and goals, lack of authority, frustration, instability, and competition among employees. Traditional responses to workplace conflict are often heavy handed, unsuccessful, and unsatisfactory.[115]

---

113   1. Randolph Lowry, J.D. Richard, and W. Meyers, Conflict Management and Counseling. Volume 29, United States of America, World, Inc., 1991, 201.

114   Ibid., 202.

115   Ibid.

In every case where conflict moves from being productive to destructive, it dramatically impacts the organization. In the United States, each year there are more than three million involuntary job terminations, and 800,000 voluntary resignations.

In response to the escalating costs of organizational conflict, and the inadequacy of existing processes to deal with it, a number of new approaches have emerged to recognize workplace conflict as normal and to view it in a calm and deliberate fashion. If we treat it as normal, conflict's impact on our emotions will be diminished and our response will be more deliberate, sophisticated and confidence-building.

One who intervenes in a neutral capacity when conflict emerges should do so with an attitude of deliberation and confidence. It is of great importance that the interviewer reflect the attitude he/she would like the people in conflict to possess.[116]

Be committed to early intervention. The sooner conflict is identified and addressed, the greater the opportunity for finding a face-saving, acceptable, and efficient way to resolve it. To establish processes for dealing with conflict, it is important whether the process will be offered informally or more formally. Informally, management's task is to make sure employees are aware of the process and know how to accept it. If formal is offered, this will include employment agreement or personal handbooks and giving employees notice of how unresolved conflict will be handled.[117]

The second new approach in managing conflict in the workplace is through collaborative negotiation. It moves from a debate on the issues to an understanding of the interests, thereby setting the stage for more creative and meaningful solutions. Its application to the workplace is based on three premises; these are legitimate alternatives to the traditional chain of command decision making process. People are capable of handling their own conflicts. Organizations can change from competitive to collaborative methods of handling conflict if processes are available that support such a move, and if top level management encourages such an approach.

---

116 Ibid., 204.
117 Ibid., 205.

Legitimate Alternatives

The 1990s came open with profound changes in the world. The most pronounced were the political and economic changes in the Soviet Union and Eastern Europe. The workplace began to recognize the value of a more participatory and cooperative approach to managing its enterprise, as well as the conflict inherent in it.

We have people better trained and more capable of resolving most of their own disputes, communicating with each other, and recognizing each other's interests, by seeking creative ways to satisfy those interests, by understanding the specifics, dealing with the people involved, and having the greatest appreciation for their needs. When trained in the process of collaborative negotiation, they can reach out and directly resolve such conflicts.[118] Entire organizations can change cultures so that such collaboration becomes the norm, both internally and externally.

It should be emphasized that just because an organization sees the benefits of a more productive and respectful approach to resolving conflict, this does not suggest that the organization should give up substantive issues that are important to it. By using collaborative negotiation, it is more likely to find workable solutions and do so in the context of respecting the relationships involved.

The third new approach to resolve conflict is mediation. This need not be part of a formal process. This can be done by the neutral third party who helps the disputants reach an agreement. Mediation is a popular tool when people seek to break an impasse in negotiations or to avoid the use of a more formal grievance procedure.[119]

Studies of mediation report that in more than ninety percent of the cases, the process can be successful. Mediation is especially effective as an alternative to litigation. Now, many employers are using mediation.

Conflict in the workplace is a reality. Traditionally, it has been handled in a way that is adversarial, and largely unproductive. New approaches suggest that more cooperative, creative, and respectful

---

118   Ibid., 208-209.
119   Ibid., 212.

processes could bring to the workplace new abilities to address inevitable conflicts and do so in an effective way.[120]

Strategies That Work

The approaches to conflict are as diverse and complex as the people involved. They dramatically affect how conflict is handled and the outcomes that are possible.

Avoidance, the most commonly used style of conflict management, reflects the belief that it is impossible to both accomplish one's personal goals and maintain relationships while in conflict. The basic strategy of avoidance is to withdraw, avoid, suppress, and deny the existence of conflict. A person using this style is shown to be unassertive, neither pursuing his/her own interests in the situation nor supporting others in achieving theirs. This person does not cooperate in defining the conflict, seeking a solution, or in carrying it out.[121]

Most of the time, church leaders will use the style of avoidance frequently for the sake of appearances. They want themselves or their congregation to look good; however, with this style, the problem will most likely resurface at some point with more intensity and a greater potential for destruction than when first identified. As an indirect method of resolution, avoidance takes the least effort in the short run, has the longest life expectancy, and has the most cost which cannot be charged back to the original conflict. It can increase the stress level, result in hostile interactions, and foster low morale.[122]

As with all approaches to conflict, avoidance can be appropriate in some instances and inappropriate in others. Some problems simply go away or are resolved by themselves. Like with all approaches, the approach of avoidance is not inherently good or bad. Wisdom is reflected in choosing it at the appropriate time.

The accommodating response to conflict is characterized by a high concern for preserving relationships, even if it means conceding

---

120   Ibid., 213.
121   Ibid.
122   Ibid.

one's own goals. Other reasons for choosing this approach might include a high need for acceptance by others, and the belief that accommodation will allow those needs to be met. The person who uses the approach of accommodation accepts the burden of responsibility for maintaining the relationship.

Accommodation, too, can be appropriate or inappropriate. We need to know when to use them. Accommodation can be both effective and ineffective in approaching conflict.

The competitive, win-or-lose style of conflict management is characterized by a very high concern for the achievement of personal goals, even at the risk of damaging or destroying the relationship. The person who chooses to use this style may not desire harm to come to the others, but he/she is willing to sacrifice almost anything to achieve personal objectives. However, people who employ the competing style do not always go head-to-head with the opposition. Sometimes they work subversively. At other times, they use the power of words to humiliate and weaken their opponents, until they finally bring them under control.[123] The challenge is not to decide whether competition is good or bad, but rather, to wisely choose when to use it.

The person with a compromising style of conflict management proposes a middle ground to others. Inherent in the compromising style is the idea of providing the other side with concessions while at the same time expecting concessions from it. This approach is based on the premise that no one can be fully satisfied, so all those involved must submit some of their personal desires to serve the common good of both parties.

The sense of compromise can have a negative connotation. Compromising integrity for personal gain, or compromising long-held beliefs for short-term advantages may be perceived as inappropriate to some in conflict. Compromise does have some very appropriate application. It allows parties to achieve some of their goals without jeopardizing relationships.

Churches utilize compromise when designing facilities, formulating budgets, and agreeing upon the ministry agenda.

---

123 Ibid.

Compromise is perceived as an effective way to handle differences by providing some of what each party needs, while maintaining sufficient relationships so the parties can continue to work together. Compromise can also be appropriately and inappropriately utilized.

The collaborative style combines a high concern for both people and objective. This approach works best when all parties are committed to the resolution of conflict.

Collaboration is not always possible or even desired; however, it holds great potential for those in conflict. A collaborative resolution of family issues can maximize the resolution of conflict and establish the possibility of an acceptable relationship in the future.

Individuals who are able to concentrate on the issues without getting caught up in negative emotions will find this style produces more satisfactory outcomes. The challenge with this approach is that it takes a great deal of time because it necessitates exploring the needs of all parties and crafting solutions that meet those needs. It also requires communication skills and a genuine commitment to resolve the conflict.

In the ministry of Jesus, He utilized a number of approaches to conflict. Jesus competed when his objective was cleaning the temple. He avoided conflict with the crowds when he retreated from them. He accommodated others in washing Mary's feet, and in the ultimate sacrifice of His life. The critical point to recognize is that people may choose from a variety of approaches to deal with conflict, and the choice will have an impact on both the way the conflict is resolved and the people involved.

As conflict is recognized, it becomes obvious that it sets the agenda for counselors and those with whom they work. Conflict presents both dangers and opportunities. It may be managed or resolved. In some cases, it sets the stage for reconciliation.

Either deliberately or passively, people have preferred ways of dealing with conflict. Behind these styles are certain attitudes that shape behavior. Our responses reflect who we are, our experiences, and our perceived values. A person who assumes conflict is basically evil will tend to avoid it. Others, who see conflict as a part of life, will take a more active role when they experience disputes.

The approaches to conflict-avoidance, accommodation, competition, compromise, and collaboration-depend on whether the individual places a higher value on maintaining good relationships, or on achieving his/her personal goals. While approaches to conflict are capable to change and combination, the five categories discussed here accurately portray the most predictable responses.

The couple going through a divorce in their marital relationship may pretend they have no reason to work toward a collaborative resolution, even concerning the children. But those who serve as resources for the family know how much they will relate to each other, even if the relationship is defined outside of the previous marriage.

Alternatively, collaboration holds great potential for those in conflict. The person with a compromising style of conflict management proposes a middle ground to others. Inherent in the compromising style is the idea of providing the other side with concessions while at the same time expecting concessions from it.

DANGER AND OPPORTUNITY IN CONFLICT RESOLUTION

Conflict occurs when competing interests clash, and that clash produces danger. Wherever there is conflict, there is the possibility that how it is handled (or not handled) will result in danger to those involved.

As people who live, work and play together, we cannot escape the reality of our differences, especially differences in our perspectives on the events and activities of our lives. Clashes are most apparent in our differences over facts, methods, values, and goals. Often conflict results from differences over what we believe to be facts. Our experiences are the same-reading, witnessing, and analyzing-but our understanding is different.

Speed Leas, one of the nationally recognized authorities on conflict in churches, suggests that conflict can be placed in one of three categories: it is substantive, stemming from the differences noted above that may be generated by a particular issue; it is interpersonal; or it is intrepersonal.[124]

A wide variety of attitudes and emotions can be expressed in a conflict. These attitudes and emotions are not inherently bad; but, conflict is capable of bringing them to the surface in a way that is not constructive. If not controlled, they can even escalate into a situation that is dangerous for those involved in the conflict, and others around them.

Conflict also has an element of opportunity, however. It presents the opportunity to change, to struggle, to grow, and to release God's power in relationships and in our world. This decade does not promise to be one in which we all work in harmony on environmental issues.[125]

While conflict may be stressful for many, change will take place because of it. Conflict also presents the opportunity for people to struggle and grow. Dr. James Mallory states in his book, The Kink and I, "Anybody that is conflict free is not experiencing growth ... the important changes in us talce place within the framework of struggle."[126]

We may not look forward to the struggle that results in growth, but we must recognize it. There's no gain without pain.

In the New Testament, the relationship of the Apostle Paul and John Mark was one of being co-workers on Paul's first missionary journey. The decision not to take John Mark on the second journey was the result of a sharp disagreement reported in Acts 15:39. One suspects that both Paul and John Mark grew through the conflict.[127]

Conflict presents the opportunity to show the power of God intervening in the lives of His people. Seeing God's hand in the resolution over and over again in the ministry of reconciliation, it is God who intervenes to dissipate anger, soften hearts, and bring people's spirits together in resolution.

---

124 1. Randolph Lowry, J.D. Richard, and W. Meyers, Conflict Management and Counseling. volume 29, United States of America, 1991.

125 John L. Walter, and Jane E. Peller, Becoming Solution-Focused in Brief Therapy, New York, NY, 1992.

126 Lowry, Richard, and Meyers.

127 Ron Kral, MS, Strategies That Work, Techniques for Solutions in Schools, 1995.

chapter five

GAINING A SATISFACTORY RESOLUTION: SUBSTANTIVE SATISFACTION, PROCEDURAL SATISFACTION AND PSYCHOLOGICAL SATISFACTION

POLITICS

The initial criterion is that of substantive satisfaction. Are the people satisfied with the substance, the terms of negotiated agreement. There must also be satisfaction with the process followed by the resolution of the dispute. Also, people who have reached a resolution must be able to look back on the process and have a feeling that they were treated in a way that will allow them to support the agreement.[128]

The Grand Old Party support for Gingrich begins to waver. The solid front of support from Republicans that House Speaker Newt Gingrich has enjoyed since he admitted to ethical lapses has started to break down. At least a half-dozen Republican House Members, from an incoming freshman to one of the party's veteran members,

---

128 Ibid., 129-131.

have hedged on their support for Gingrich in the last few days, saying they want to wait for the

House Ethics Committee to act before they decide whether to vote for his reelection as speaker.[129]

Gingrich acknowledged on December 21st that he had provided the committee with inaccurate, incomplete, and unreliable statements about a course that was to be taught at two small colleges in Georgia. At issue is whether he improperly used the tax exempt programs for partisan purposes, a charge that Gingrich had denied until a week ago.

The 105th Congress convenes January 7 and one of its first matters will be the election of a Speaker. The Republican majority had decided in November to make Gingrich the first Republican in nearly seventy years to be reelected to the office, but since then, the ethics accusation have cast a cloud over the formal vote.[130]

Republican Marge 'Roukeman, an eight-term Republican and the dean of the New Jersey delegation, states she will not prejudge, one way or the other. The jury is still out until the Ethics Committee makes their recommendation. The chairman of the committee, Republican Nancy Johnson, has said her panel will decide on Gingrich's punishment before January 7. Republican-Elect John I. Rune, R.S.D., the liaison for the freshman class with the House leadership, states it is to premature, too far out in front at this point.[131]

The penalty could be as severe as expulsion from the House or sanctions, either of which would cost him his job as Speaker. Or the penalty might be as mild as a reprimand, the equivalent of a scolding, which would allow him to remain as speaker.

Gingrich and the Republicans, for political reasons, would like to have the conflict completed as quickly as possible. However the Democrats, for equally politically reasons, would like to keep the political conflict over the Republican leader and his reelection for some time, keeping the issue at the front of public attention and trying to erode support for Gingrich within his own ranks.[132] Democrats

129 New York Times News Service, 2 and 3A.
130 Ibid.
131 Ibid., 3.
132 Ibid.

want to keep the Republican Party under increasing pressure to settle Newt Gingrich's ethics troubles before costing a vote reelecting him as Speaker.

Meanwhile, The New York Times conservative columnist William Safire, who has called for the Speaker to step down, said on a Sunday morning talk show that Gingrich is comparing himself to Richard Nixon in 1952, and plans to weather out the storm. In a separate appearance, former federal judge and U.S. Supreme Court nominee Robert Bock, a conservative Republican, also said Gingrich should consider stepping aside because he will not be able to effectively advocate conservative G.O.P. causes.

House Ethics Committee Chairwoman Nancy Johnson (R.-Conn.) Reportedly is hoping to hammer out a schedule today for the committee to reconvene and complete its work in the Gingrich case before the January 7 vote on the speakership. During the hearing, outside counsel James M. Cole, who has conducted the ethics probe, is expected to outline his findings against the speaker. Cole's summary is expected to reveal far more details than those contained in the negotiated twenty-two page report issued by an ethics subcommittee two weeks ago, and agreed to by Gingrich.

Although Republicans initially demurred on whether those hearings should be public, they offered a unified call for open hearings in Sunday appearances. In an appearance on Fox News Sunday, Representative John Linder states there ought to be a public hearing and let everything in the Ethics Committee report be released to the public.

Democratic Congressional Campaign Committee Chairman Martin Frost (D. Texas), appearing to Meet the Press, also called for a public airing of the findings against Gingrich, but he suggested that they will result in the Speaker's removal. This is a matter of the integrity of the House, Frost said, we're not trying to have a Democratic Speaker. Republicans won the election. They are entitled to a Republican Speaker.

Following Frost on Meet the Press, Safice warned that prolonging the ethics case could weaken the Republican causes. He called on Gingrich to let the Congress off the hook and resign as Speaker.

After a more than two year struggle, the primary House ethics case against Speaker Newt Gingrich is scheduled to come to a close exactly three weeks from today. Between now and then, however, House Republicans will be asked to stand by Gingrich and reelect him as Speaker on Tuesday. While casting such a vote has made some members uncomfortable, the Speaker received two influential endorsements on New Year's Eve that will likely end any resistance and signal that the Speaker is likely to receive the lightest punishment for his ethics violation.[133]

At the meeting, which will be closed to the public, the members are scheduled to vote to accept the findings of the House Investigative Sub-Committee and Gingrich's decision to admit to the charges rather than face a public hearing to determine his culpability. Members of the United States House of Representatives, on Tuesday, imposed an unprecedented sanction on Speaker Newt Gingrich for ethics violations, and Republicans braced for an uncertain future with their battered leader. On a 395-28 vote, the House accepted an ethics committee recommendation that Gingrich receive a formal reprimand and a $300,000.00 fine for his admitted violations. Gingrich is the first Speaker to be reprimanded while in office.

The vote marks the conclusion of an ethics probe that began in September 1993, but it may not signal an end to Gingrich's troubles. The Speaker must mend his relationship with a House Republican conference that is more skeptical and less forgiving than the one he led into power in 1994. However, two days after receiving an unprecedented sanction for ethics violations, House Speaker Newt Gingrich held a news conference to talk about a balanced budget amendment and take the first step toward what he hopes will be political recovery. But even as the Speaker moved to repair his public image, the two-year ethics investigation into his activities left several legal questions that are unlikely to be resolved in the near future.

Mr. Gingrich had a more combative than apologetic during appearances at three town meetings in his suburban Atlanta District.

---

133   Cummings Jeanne, Cox News Service. The Lufkin Daily News. 1-A.

He blamed his former lawyer for the submission of misleading documents to the House Ethics Committee.[134]

Mr. Gingrich stated he made a mistake, and he had stated this. Sometimes this is not enough for some people-saying I made a mistake; I am very sorry. Now let's get on with the business and our lives. However, this does not work quite that way. A lot of lives and feelings are involved in a situation like this.

William Lincola says the usual response in situations of conflict is to define the issues, and then react to them. He also states that interests relate to needs. Interests are always present and very real to the people involved. The need for recognition is an example of an interest. From time to time, one needs to be told that they are important to the family, to the church, or that the hard work is noticed.[135] In looking at recognition as an interest, how such issues are handled will determine if our interest in recognition is met.

Making a clear distinction between the interests and the issues is essential in understanding conflict and its resolution. However, when conflict occurs, the issues usually are not easily identified. The interests hold the key to resolution.[136]

Seeking reasons for positions when issues are raised, they are usually defined by the person's positions relating to them. If the issue is planning a family vacation, it may be defined by family members taking positions on where each wants to go. Reactions to these positions can immediately cause disagreement or delay, or prevent a discussion of important interests. Interest based problem solving is only accomplished when people seek what is behind such positions.[137]

Ask questions. The Gospels have described a number of instances when Jesus opted to ask question or make gentle statements, rather than engage in criticism or argument.

Being alert to the unstated. We do not have the ability and power to look into people's minds, as Christ did, but we can be aware of both their stated and unstated communication. Sensitivity to what is left

---

134 Washington Post, in The Lufkin Daily News, 6-A.
135 Lowry, Richard, and Meyers, 89.
136 Ibid., 90.
137 Ibid., 91.

unstated will assist in identifying the interests of the people involved, even if they carmot, or will not, verbalize those interests themselves. A common example of unstated communication is one's unwillingness to express need for recognition.[138]

Benefits can result from discovering common interests and using them as a basis to forge new, creative solutions. Different interests can often contribute more to conflict resolution than do the common interests.

To achieve creative solutions, people must first recognize that their perceptions dramatically limit their choices. People must go beyond the obvious, past the certain and into the realm of increased possibilities, rather than argue over shallow conclusions.[139]

Creative thinking is to develop or assess the list of options to determine which are indeed possible. The focus should be on the potential of each solution, not its desirability.

Resolving conflict, or assisting others who need assistance in doing so, requires substantial creativity. An agreement reached in negotiation will always be compared with disputant's other alternatives.

HOW TO DEAL WITH THE ISSUE OF DIVORCE PRE, DURING, AND POST

We know this is not a perfect world. Even with the best efforts of counselors, therapists, ministers, and friends, a substantial number of marriages are going to be fractured, ending in divorce. The impact of the event will be long lasting; in most cases, its effect will be felt by everyone in the original family for a lifetime.[140]

With divorce comes an erosion of commitments to our partners and to the institution of marriage itself; with divorce comes a weakening of unspoken moral commitments to the children. Today,

138   Ibid., 93.
139   Ibid., 95.
140   Ibid., 173.

people expect more from the marriage than previous generations did, and people are respecting it less, at this time.

While acknowledging that the legal system has done what it does fairly well. However, there are significant movements in both secular and religious institutions to effectively deal with what seems to be the inevitability of divorce.

It is such a circumstance that the advantages of the mediation alternative are most evident. Financial costs for lawyers are dramatically decreased; settlements are more creative because the divorcing couple has more latitude in coming up with solutions best suited to the personal situation. Divorcing couples have a greater commitment to the argument, there seems to be a strong correlation between the process used to establish the obligation and its fulfillment.

Relationships are treated with greater respect-not because the conflict is less acute, but because the environment in which it is handled promotes respect. The traditional response to that concern has been to sever all relationships with the divorcing couple and their family, so that what one believes about the commitment to marriage is not misinterpreted.[141]

First is the reality that those who are divorcing are just as governed by Paul's writings to the Corinthians as others in the Christian community. "If any of you have had a dispute with another, dare he take it before the ungodly for judgment instead of before the saints."[142] "The very fact that you have lawsuits among you means you have been completely defeated already."[143]

A couple can choose not to go to court for getting a divorce. One option can be secular mediation. Structured either through the court or through private practitioners, it is better than courtroom litigation. It can bring financial savings and a respectful environment, as well as foster a creative outcome. Even secular mediation falls short of what could be available in the Christian community.[144]

---

141   Ibid., 175-176.
142   Holy Bible, I Corinthians 6:1.
143   Ibid., 6:7.
144   Lowery, Richard, and Meyers, 174-175.

Occasionally, such reconciliation might take place, so divorce is avoided. More often, it would encourage reconciliation of the people after the divorce has occurred.

Reconciliation may not bring back a marriage, but can allow the former spouses to co-exist in the world together. So often, a couple within a church in seeking a divorce, one or both spouses leave the congregation. In doing so, the spouses leave some of their closest friends, the people to whom they would have turned with any other problem, and those with whom they were close to and shared a spiritual relationship.[145]

In our Christian community, we need to assist people who are moving through a divorce. Such a process would help avoid the secular courts and establish the possibility for reconciliation, but this would offer a less comfortable involvement for church members. Others might say there is potential for mediation of divorces within the Christian community this way. We are all called to care for people on every level, physical, financial, spiritual and so-forth.

Conflict management assistance can be most beneficial in the context of life long family relationships, areas of important personal concerns, and an environment of great emotion reflecting only minimal preparation. Through counseling, innovative conflict management, and even divorce mediation, the family can be a more functional and supportive entity.[146]

---

145 Ibid., 177.
146 Ibid., 177-178.

IMPACT OF DIVORCE ON CHILDREN AT VARIOUS STAGES OF THEIR DEVELOPMENT

The disruption of a family by divorce appears to cause serious trouble not because of one factor, but because of a collection of factors which, together, exceed some children's tolerance of stress. The younger the child, the more severe the impact.

Boys seem to have more adjustment problems than girls. Boys may suffer more from the lack of contact with the father than the girls. Children are often better adjusted when in the custody of the parents of the same sex rather than the parent of the opposite sex. Joint custody seems to show better results than sole custody, due to the fact that joint custody results in less geographic mobility and a more equitable financial situation, which minimizes stress factors for divorced families.

Those families where the father continues to be close to his children, due to lengthy visitations, show the best results for children. Those fathers who no longer have intense animosity toward their ex-wives, those who are economically secure and better educated, those who are lonely but not depressed, and those whose children express pleasure in the visits (more often younger children) seem most likely to be able to sustain this close relationship. Parental conflict, both expressed in anger and repressed in tension, predicts damage to children better than does family structure, married or divorced.

VALUE OF MEDIATION

As people consider reconciliation, it is helpful to remind them that God can intervene and be part of the process. God loves His children and the church, and He wants His people to be reconciled. Given the opportunity to speak to his people through prayer, God will ready their hearts for the reconciliation process.

A person cannot enter into a process to successfully resolve conflict without a certain amount of preparation. There must be a transition from the state of conflict to a readiness for resolution.[147]

By helping people prepare for reconciliation, the mediator assists them in making the transition from investing in the conflict to investing in the resolution. Once that transition is complete, they will be ready for someone to minister to them. They are reminded once again of those values that are so easy to forget in the heat of battle.[148]

There should always be some ground rules in a mediation session. However, it is hard but not uncommon for the mediator to spend several minutes describing these ground rules.

The disputants rarely hear such admonitions. They are anxiously waiting to tell their side of the story, eager to proclaim the errors of their adversary and describe how the problem ought to be resolved. Most of the time they are chomping at the bit to express their feelings about the matter at hand.

Communication in conflict resolution operates in two ways, speaking and listening. It is critically important for the two sides to hear each other, to listen carefully.

In the Christian context, the two sides may also communicate with each other through prayer to God. When people who are in conflict get down on their knees together and pray about the conflict, a kind of softening talces place.[149]

The Lord does intervene through prayer. People enmeshed in conflict communicate and listen to each other very carefully as they

---

147 Ibid., 109.
148 Ibid., 109-110.
149 Ibid., 111.

pray. There is something healing about this process. In the church, we have the unique opportunity to utilize the dynamic power of prayer, and also through that mechanism to talk with each other in meaningful, unique, and helpful ways.

Parties know what the dispute is about and are able to identify those tangible items. Identifying the issues is a reasonably easy task. Setting the agenda is not hard, but very important, because it can diminish uncertainty and provides direction for successfully conducting the session.

While the issues are easily identified in most conflicts, the interests may be hidden. People can bring to the table underlying needs which may be difficult for them to admit or describe. Yet such needs is essential in resolving the conflict.[150]

The people that are involved in the conflict create options that will meet their interests. Options must include thoughts on how the solution will be put into place. Often, people in strong acute conflict can see a solution, but do not know how to back off from the position and accept it.

The mediation process must include a phase of closure and settlement. Jesus always found Himself at the point of closure. There was always a sense of closure with Him, a sense that he was saying, "Here is my ministry to you-my miracle that involves you. Here is my teaching to you." He brought the session to closure by forcing those involved to think about the reality of acceptance and rejection.[151]

---

150 Ibid., 112.
151 Ibid., 116.

CHARACTERISTICS A MEDIATOR CAN USE TO HELP PEOPLE RESOLVE CONFLICT INTERESTS, PERCEPTIONS, VALUES, HISTORY, AND CREDIBILITY

Fisher and Brown suggest that we focus our understanding to the building blocks of relationships.[152] We need to examine the concept of interests, and show how they may be most commonly thought of as needs-needs that are not always tangible, concrete, and easy to define, but are very real to the individual. Since needs drive conflict, they usually must be understood and addressed before conflict is resolved.[153] It is very important for us to point out that disputants who have a greater understanding of their opponent's needs, goals, and motivations will be in a far more powerful position by offering solutions that are more responsive and thus resolve the differences between the two sides.[154]

A dispute between a family member and the parent is a way of showing how understanding can help two people resolve their conflict. By not arguing and responding negatively to the situation and seeking to understand each other's interests in the matter, the two may come up with a number of ways to resolve the differences, short of arguing. The issue causes them to argue, but understanding the interests causes them to be creative in finding a solution.

In addition to interests, one must understand perception. This is the style of viewing a situation or circumstance. Most people view the

---

152 Ibid., 72.
153 Ibid.
154 Ibid.

same situation from a perspective that reflects their own experience, background, and goals.[155]

Several people viewing a situation will view the same objects quite differently, and their descriptions of those objects have great diversity. To one, the objects were characterized as highway hazards; to another, the same items were renewable resources; to a third, they were testament to God.[156] They were describing trees. To the engineers, who wanted to remove them for road construction, they were highway hazards. To the timber industry, they were renewable resources. To the naturalists, they were testaments to God.. Understanding perceptions is critical in building productive relationships.[157]

In addition to interests and perceptions, we need to understand values. Different values may impact the relationship. Values can and may reflect our basic characters and the importance we attach to specific personal characteristics; however, shared values become a resource the counselors can draw upon to help people manage conflict. When individuals involved in conflict have different values, especially values related to culture or religion, they can be great impediments to successful dispute resolution.

The Institute for Dispute Resolution is studying the contrast in seeing how conflict related to mass disasters-airplane crashes-is handled in our different cultures. In the study, they discovered the contrast in the values exhibited after the August 1985 crash of a Delta jumbo jet in Dallas, Texas, following by the crash of a Japan Air Lines jumbo jet in Japan ten days later. After the Japan Air Lines disaster, the president of the company resigned, then made a personal visit to apologize to each family who had lost someone in the crash. Also, the airline made settlement payments to each family within a few months after the accident, and, reflecting the values of the culture, no lawsuits were filed in Japan by the families of Japanese victims.[158]

In contrast, after the Delta crash, responsibility was denied by the airline. While some cash settlements were offered, Delta's insurers

---

155   Ibid., 73.
156   Ibid.
157   Ibid.
158   Ibid., 74.

took a highly adversarial stance in the ensuing litigation. Years later, litigation still continues at the federal appellate court level.[159]

The Japanese value a sense of relationship, and they do not want anything to fracture their community. With this dedicated feeling and with the willingness to show responsibility and accountability, they have values which could protect the community from divisive actions.

To contrast the Americans, Delta Airlines seem to value a frontier style approach to justice by believing that conflict should be resolved adversarially. So providing that kind of mechanism has become a priority for us, even though it can fracture relationships. By putting the burden on the side bringing the action to demonstrate the responsibility of the other, as opposed to accepting the responsibility as our fault, the natural response is to defend against that.[160]

Values, who we are and how we prioritize basic personal characteristics, influence the willingness to resolve conflict. It is essential that consideration of values must be part of effective conflict resolution.

Understanding the history of the people involved in conflict is very important. History provides a context from which their interests, perceptions, and values flow. Our background history can play an important part in the characteristics of our interests, perceptions and values in our everyday conflict in life. When the history is understood, the explained behavior can help the counselor understand its impact on the process of reconciliation.

Another component of relationships is credibility. By the time most conflicts have impacted relationships, whatever credibility a person had with the other has dissipated. Credibility is very important and necessary if people are to trust, have confidence in, and be able to rely upon each other.

All of us have experienced moments when we question the ability to trust another person, or on the other hand, as we move through life, our basic presumptions of how people will handle or respond to different circumstances may be confirmed or denied.

---

159   Ibid.
160   Ibid., 75.

The text gives us a good example of showing credibility, the ability to be trusted. This is stated as a family is driving in the cold, snowy January night in Minnesota on their way to Oregon. In Northern Idaho, the family discovered they would need tire chains in order to cross over the steep Fourth of July Pass. Before getting to this location, the family stopped in a small, one-bay service station. The family found the station attendant sleeping in his car. The attendant did put the chains on the tires. As he finished the task, the family paid in cash, with the thought he would probably keep the cash without ringing up the sale. However, the attendant methodically wrote up the ticket and placed the substantial cash payment in the register. Without knowing him well, the family left feeling much better about how the attendant might have installed the chains, based upon how he handled the money. In a matter of moments, the attendant had demonstrated his trustworthiness, a value of providing the basis of good working relationships.[161]

Consistent message-one day we could receive a message, and the next day stringent conditions could make such a message given impossible. Regardless of the ultimate outcome, messages and their actions lend virtual credibility to the situation.

Predictable consequences-credibility is built on predictable consequences. Predictability stems from a history of encounters and from the consistency of actions with words. Whether the consequences are positive or negative, when they are predictable, they become something to be dealt with in resolving conflict.[162]

Forgiveness necessitates a decision to slice out part of our history-that event, that action which breached our relationship with the other person involved. We may not forget it, but we can decide that it will not preclude our future relationship.

Finally, forgiveness involves beginning again. It may not be immediate. It may not be quick, and the relationship may be rebuilt in a different way than it was before the conflict. Nevertheless, a

---

161 Ibid., 76-77.
162 Ibid.

rebuilding process begins that can ultimately lead to reconciliation and a renewed relationship.[163]

The last characteristic that sets the stage for reconciliation is sacrifice. Marriage and family counselors encourage commitment and sacrifice as the basis for a strong family. Turning to the scriptures, we find numerous examples of sacrifice and its impact on human relationships.

Reconciliation does not take place in a vacuum. It stems from the relationship of those involved. While those relationships reflect the diversity of the people in them, the attributes necessary for effectively resolving differences are identifiable. When a relationship is established through acceptance, communication, understanding, credibility, forgiveness, and sacrifice, it has established that possibility.[164]

THE ACADEMY OF FAMILY MEDIATORS

Training to Become a Mediator

The Academy of Family Mediators was established in 1981 as a non-profit educational membership association and is the largest family mediation organization in existence. Members are mediators working in a variety of settings, including private practice, courts, school, and government in the United States and internationally.[165]

Members of the Academy of Family Mediators provide mediation services to families facing decisions involving separation, divorce or marital dissolution, child custody, parenting, visitation, property division, wills and estates, elder care, spouse support or alimony, child support, family business, pre-nuptial agreements, and many

---

163 Ibid., 79.
164 Ibid., 80-82.
165 Material found on Internet under Academy of Family Mediators, 4 Militia Drive, Lexington, MA 02173, 1 of 1.

other disputes, conflicts or issues involving the family. The Academy of Family Mediators can refer you to a mediator in your area and provide information about mediation training. Academy of Family Mediators also holds annual and special conferences for mediators and has a wide selection of educational materials, books, videotapes, audio tapes and professional publications.[166]

Although mediators may come from a variety of professional backgrounds, including attorneys, psychologists, social workers, marriage or family counselors, clergy people, accountants and financial specialists, they received specialized training to become mediators.

- Membership
- Referrals to mediators
- Conferences
- Bookstore and educational materials
- Mediation training
- Mediator insurance
- Academy of Family Mediators publications
- Internship opportunities
- Frequently asked questions.[167]

The first thing in becoming a mediator is to attend a basic mediation skills training course. The Academy of Family Mediators approves training programs in the areas of family and divorce mediation, which must be at least 30 hours and 40 hours long, respectfully. The academy can provide you with a complete listing of approved training programs.

Most mediators who successfully break into the field continue to take as much training as possible in all areas of mediation skills, substantive knowledge abut such things as pensions, domestic violence, child development, and much more. Attending an academy conference is an excellent way to continue to develop your skills and network with other mediators.[168]

---

166   Ibid., 1 of 5.
167   Ibid.
168   Ibid., 2 of 5.

Networking is extremely important. The more mediators with whom you interact, the more you learn and the more opportunities you hear about. Get involved in a local or statewide mediation organization, locate an opportunity to apprentice with an established mediator, attend academy conferences, and be creative in developing your own opportunities. The academy can provide you with a list of mediators in your area.[169]

The Academy of Family Mediators can provide you with a listing of training programs, which have met the core requirements for training, that have been established by the academy. Divorce mediation training programs must be at least 40 hours in length, while training programs in family mediation custody, parenting, and other family issues, are required to be at least 30 hours in length.

Costs vary depending on the type, length, and location of the training and who the trainers are. The cost of a training program is usually comparable to a four credit graduate course.[170] Some states and courts are offering certification for mediators.

Completing a training program alone does not provide certification. Many mediators in private practice have combined a mediation practice with the practice of their profession of origin, at least when starting out. Developing a full time mediation practice takes a lot of hard work and may take several years, or longer.

At the high end of the income scale for a well established, experienced family mediator in full time private practice could be in the $40-50,000 range. Most mediators also earn income from other sources, such as teaching, training, or from their profession of origin.[171]

The academy recommends that mediators have completed a basic mediation training course to start and then continue to take additional training. If you are involved in a divorce or another family issue that is filed in court, any agreement you reach may be filed with the court. If the dispute is not filed in court, the agreement is usually considered to be a contract. Depending on the nature of the agreement and the

---

169 Ibid.
170 Ibid.
171 Ibid., 3 of 5.

dispute, if there is a breach of the contract, you might be able to file a claim with the court. At this time, the mediator may recommend to contact a lawyer for any questions about this before or during a mediation.[172]

Mediated agreements have been found to be adhered to more often than judgements by the court. This makes sense if you know that no agreement may be reached in mediation unless everyone involved agrees.

Mediation is a private process, not open to the public. For the most part, mediation is confidential. However, there may be certain limitations to confidentiality, depending on state law or other factors. These limitations should definitely be discussed with the mediator or a lawyer before you begin mediation. If the case is filed in court, disclosure of the terms of the agreement may be required.[173]

When obtaining a divorce using a mediator, it must be filed in court. However, a mutually agreeable resolution to all of the property, financial, custody, parenting and other issues to resolve, and the court accepts the settlement, it is unlikely that many court appearances are made. The more one can do outside of the court, the better.[174]

When using mediation for other types of family issues, one may never need to go to court. In divorce cases, mediators will recommend that each spouse be represented by their own attorney. However, by using mediation fewer legal services are needed, and those used will be different than if not using mediation.

The lawyer will provide guidance and legal counsel and will draft documents for filing with the court. Even if the mediator is a lawyer, the mediator is not acting as a lawyer and cannot represent either person in the divorce.[175]

One can find a mediator by requesting a referral from the Academy of Family Mediators. The academy will provide names of mediators in that area who have met stringent training and experience requirements set by the academy.

---

172 Ibid.
173 Ibid.
174 Ibid., 4 of 5.
175 Ibid.

When choosing a mediator, it is just like any other professional, such as a physician, lawyer, or accountant. Generally obtain the following information: training, experience, and background of the mediator, experience in a particular type of dispute, fees charged and how fees are divided among the parties to the mediation, and professional memberships. Find out whether the mediator is certified. Certification is available only in certain states.[176]

The cost of mediation can vary tremendously, depending on where you live, whether the mediator is in private practice or works in a court or community mediation program. Asking about fees up front is best.

Anyone who has an interest in family mediation is welcome to join the Academy of Family Mediators. No training is required to join the Academy of Family Mediators; however, to become a practitioner member or consultant member of the academy, certain training and experience requirements must be met.[177]

---

176 Ibid.
177 Ibid., 5 of 5.

chapter six

GOD TAILORS THE EVENTS OF OUR LIVES

The more you trust God, the easier it is to do His will. This is especially true when you are involved in conflict. If you believe God is watching over you with perfect love and unlimited power, you will be able to serve Him faithfully as a peacemaker, even in the most difficult circumstances.[178]

The fact that God has ultimate control of all things does not release us from responsibility for our actions. In both Matthew 12:36 and Romans 14:12, we are reminded that He has allowed us to exercise immediate control of ourselves, and He will hold us fully accountable for the decisions we make in life.[179] Knowledge of our sovereignty of God should motivate us to be even more responsible. As the passages cited above indicate, nothing in our lives happens by chance. We will never suffer trials or be involved in disputes unless God allows it. In other words, every conflict that comes into our lives has somehow been ordained by God. Knowing that He has personally tailored the events of our lives should dramatically affect how we respond to them.[180]

By allowing us to suffer insults, conflict, and other hardships, God teaches us to rely more on Him.[181] He also allows us to suffer the unpleasant consequences of our sins so we will see our need for

---

178 Ken Sande, The Peacemaker, 9th Printing, Scripture quotations are from the New International Version, U.S.A.: Zondervan Bible Publisher, 1996, 43.

179 New American Standard Bible, Matthew 12:36 and Romans 14:12.

180 Sande., 45-46.

181 New American Standard Bible, 2 Cor. 1:9; 12:7-10.

repentance.[182] In addition, God uses difficulties to conform us to the likeness of Christ.[183]

When you are involved in conflict, you, too, must decide whether or not you will trust God. Trusting God does not mean believing He will do all that you want, but rather, He will do everything He knows is good. If you do not trust God, you will inevitably place your trust in yourself or someone else, which ultimately leads to grief. On the other hand, if you believe God is sovereign and He will never let anything into your life unless it can be used for good, you will see conflicts not as accidents, but as assignments. This kind of trust glorifies God and inspires the faithfulness needed for effective peacemaking.[184]

If you are presently involved in conflict, the following questions will help you apply the principals presented in this chapter.

1. Have you been looking at this dispute as something that happened by chance, as something done to you by someone else, or as something that god allowed in your life for a specific purpose?

2. What questions, doubts, or fears do you have because of this dispute?

3. Read Psalms 37 and 73. What do these psalms warn you not to do? What do they instruct you to do? What comforting promises do they provide?

4. How would your feelings, attitude, and behavior change if you started seeing this dispute as an assignment from a perfectly loving and all-powerful God?

5. What good might God bring about if you respond to this conflict in a biblical manner?[185]

Conflicts generally involve two types of issues: material and personal. Material issues involve substantive matters that must be resolved to settle disagreements.

---

182 Ibid., Psa. 119:67-71.
183 Ibid. Rom. 8:28-29.
184 Sande, 54-55.
185 Ibid., 61.

Some disputes involve only personal issues and others only material issues. In most conflicts, however, both types are present. In which case, the personal issues often have a strong influence on how we will deal with the material issues.

One of the first things to do when you are involved in a conflict is to define the personal and material issues and discern how they relate to one another. Once you have a clear understanding of these dynamics, you can begin to decide which steps you must take to resolve the problem. It is usually wise to begin the process by asking yourself whether this is really worth fighting over? When significant personal or material issues are involved, the answer to this question will be yes. However, if the situation is viewed from a biblical perspective, the answer will be no, which means one should settle the matter as quickly and quietly as possible.

In many situations, the best way to resolve conflict is simply to overlook the offenses of others. When we overlook the wrongs others commit against us, we are imitating God's extraordinary forgiveness toward us. The scriptures provide us with the following examples:

- A man's wisdom gives him patience, it is to his glory to overlook an offense (Proverbs 19:11; Cf 12:16; 15:18; 20:03).
- Starting a quarrel is like breaching a dam; so drop the matter before a dispute breaks out (Proverbs 17:14; Cf 26:17).
- Above all, love each other deeply, because loves covers over a multitude ofsins(IPeter4;8; Cf. Proverbs 10:12; 17:9).
- Be completely humble and gentle; be patient, bearing with one another in love (Eph. 4:2).
- Bear with each other and forgive whatever grievances you may have against one another. Forgive as the Lord forgave you (Col. 3:13; Cf. Eph. 4:32).[186]

When placing the focus on God, through prayer, you can begin to experience something that does not seem logical. The hostility,

---

186 Ibid., 63.

anxiety, and inner conflict with which you have been dealing will begin to give way to a peace so unexpected that Paul said it would transcend all understanding. Although this peace may be only internal at first, it will often grow into an external peace-or reconciliation that will likewise surpass the comprehension of those who have been in the conflict.[187]

---

187   Ibid., 67.

CONCLUSION

Conflict arises from a discord of needs, drives, wishes, and/or demands. Conflict in and of itself is not positive or negative. Rather, it is the response to conflict that transforms it into either a competitive, destructive experience or a constructive challenge offering the opportunity for growth. Since conflict is an inevitable part of life, learning and understanding conflict resolution defines conflict as a natural condition and examines the origins of conflict, responses to conflict, and outcomes of those responses. It presents the essential principles, foundation, abilities and problem solving processes of conflict resolution, discusses the elements of conflict resolution, and introduces four approaches toward implementing conflict resolution.

Conflict provides opportunities to glorify God, to serve others, and to grow to be like Christ. These opportunities, which are sometimes described as being faithful to God, merciful to others, and acting justly ourselves, are mentioned throughout Scripture. Jesus teaches us to pay attention to "the more important matter of the law—justice, mercy, and faithfulness."[188] As you pursue these opportunities, with God's help, you can use conflict as a stepping stone to a closer relationship with God and a more fulfilling and fruitful Christian life.

People look at conflict in different ways. To some, conflict is an unpleasant inconvenience that they should put behind them as quickly as possible. To others, conflict is a hazard that threatens to sweep them off their feet and leave them bruised and hurting. But a few people see conflict as an opportunity to solve common problems in a way that honors God and benefits everyone involved.[189]

188 New International Version, Matthew 23:23, 27.
189 Ibid., 16.

The way we look at conflict strongly influences the way we respond to it. People who believe that conflict is wrong and dangerous are uncomfortable with personal differences of any kind, and they will usually do everything they can to avoid controversy. However, when they can no longer ignore, cover up, or run away from a conflict, they sometimes go to the other extreme. Feeling backed into a corner and not knowing how to deal with the situation constructively, they may become overly defensive and lash out at those around them.

People who see conflict as an inconvenience want to get through it as quickly as possible, so they often pursue impulsive and superficial solutions. This approach may work well with minor disagreements, but when serious issues are involved, it often creates more problems than it solves.

Others believe conflict is inherently neutral, that it is neither good nor bad. The approach is in a purely objective manner. They avoid making moral evaluations of attitudes and actions of the people involved. Instead of dealing with uncomfortable moral questions, they focus on improving communication and finding a settlement that satisfies as many people as possible. In the process, underlying problems often are overlooked.

There are people who view conflict as a contest. They see it as an opportunity to assert their rights, to control others, and to take advantage of their situation. People like this generally make little effort to avoid disagreements, or to overlook minor offenses.

Once a dispute starts, they keep pressing the matter as long as there is any chance they might win. These people often are very aware of the wrongs of others, but they usually find it difficult to admit or see their own wrongs. Typically, winning a dispute means more to them than preserving a relationship.

Many people are ambivalent toward conflict. Their views and responses fluctuate according to their moods and the type of situation. In many cases, they will try to avoid controversy. However, they might turn a minor difference of opinion into a major argument.

We have five styles of conflict management. First is avoiding, wanting to protect ourselves from unpleasant discussions, we either deny that there is a conflict, or simply refuse to deal with it. Avoiding a conflict only postpones needed discussion, produces frustration, and leads to more complicated problems.[190]

Second is accommodating. This style is appropriate when the issues are unimportant compared to the value of the relationship, or when we believe we may be in the wrong. In other cases this may give others a sense of vindication, even when they are in the wrong, which may lead to future conflicts.[191]

Third is compromising. Believing there is no way to find a better solution, we meet others halfway, allowing them to prevail on certain issues while we prevail on others. This style is appropriate when no sin of evil intent is involved, when it is difficult to determine a clear-cut solution, and when a standoff may cause greater harm than splitting the difference.[192]

Fourth is competing. Assuming that there are only two possible outcomes to conflict, winning and losing, we do all we can to win by imposing our will and our solutions on others. This style requires us to be aggressive, domineering, and uncooperative in the pursuit of alternative solutions. While competing may be necessary when quick, vital solutions are needed or when we are defending important moral principles, this style produces unsatisfactory solutions, promotes hostility, and damages relationships.

Fifth, and most effective of all, is accepting that teamwork is most productive; we make a sincere effort to work with others in developing mutually satisfactory solutions to our problems. This style usually requires effective communication skills, determination, and flexibility. Collaborating can still result in deficient solutions; but generally focuses on the interests of the people involved, not on God's interest. Because this style usually fails to deal biblically with the underlying causes of conflict, collaborating, too, sometimes produces incomplete solutions and leaves the door open for further controversy.

---

190   Sande, 17.
191   Ibid., 18.
192   Ibid., 19.

Any time we leave God out of the picture and disregard His commands to deal with the underlying causes of conflict, it is more difficult to resolve disputes and restore genuine peace.[193]

As God opens our hearts, we confess our sins and forgive each other, then we can feel the conflict moving out of the situation. Many of the problems associated with the approaches to conflict can be prevented if we learn to look at conflict biblically.[194]

The Bible does not teach that all conflict is bad; instead, it teaches that some differences are natural and beneficial. As human beings, we all have different opinions, desires, perspectives, and priorities, which are not inherently right or wrong; they are simply the results of God-given diversity and personal preferences. When handled properly, disagreements in these areas can stimulate production.

Not all conflict is neutral or beneficial. The Bible teaches that many disagreements are the direct result of sinful motives and behavior.

The Bible teaches we should see conflict as an opportunity to demonstrate the presence and power of God. Conflict always provides an opportunity to glorify God, that is, to show Him honor and bring Him praise. In particular, conflict gives you a chance to show God that you love, respect, and trust Him. At the same time, it allows you to show others that God is loving, wise, powerful and faithful.

You can do this in several ways. You can trust God; you can acknowledge God, and you can obey God. Every time you encounter a conflict, you have an opportunity to show what you really think of God. If we hold to His commands, we will show that we love Him with all our hearts and with all our soul and with all our mind.[195] This honors God and shows others how worthy He is of our devotion.

Most conflict will provide an opportunity to become more Christ-like. God's highest purpose for us is making us comfortable, wealthy, and happy. If we have put our faith in Him, He has something far more wonderful in mind for us.

---

193 Ibid.
194 Ibid.
195 New International Version, Matthew 22:37, 22.

Conflict is one of the many tools that God can use to help us develop a more Christlike character. To begin with, He may use conflict to remind us of our weakness and to encourage us to depend more on Him.[196] The more we depend on His wisdom and power, the more we will be imitating the Lord Jesus.[197]

When involved in conflict, we might ask ourselves these questions:

1. Summarize the dispute by placing events in chronological order. Describe what is being done to resolve the dispute.
2. What has made this dispute worse?
3. What are the primary goals as the dispute is being resolved?
4. Which style of conflict management is being used?
5. How can we glorify God, please and honor Him throughout the conflict?
6. How can we serve others?
7. How can we grow more like Christ through conflict?
8. What guidance has taken place in the situation, such as feelings, personal opinions about what is right, or what is taught to us in the Bible?
9. What is the most struggling part at the time of the conflict? Controlling the fear of what is going to happen, a lack of support from others?
10. All of these are good questions to ask. Also, another one could be if God were to evaluate the conflict, how would you like for Him to handle the situation?

If it is possible, as far as it depends on you, live at peace with everyone.[198] The Bible tells us, "Trust in the Lord with all your heart and lean not on your own understanding; in all your ways acknowledge Him, and He will make your paths straight."[199]

---

196 Ibid., 2 Corinthians 12:7-10.
197 Ibid., Luke 22:41-44, 25.
198 Ibid., Proverbs 12:18, 29.
199 Ibid., 3:5-6, 101.

One of the greatest truths of the Bible is that God is concerned about every area of our lives, including our jobs. He loves us and He has a plan for us. That is why the Bible urges us to cast all of our anxiety on Him because He cares for us.[200]

---

200   Ibid., I Peter 5:7.

BIBLIOGRAPHY

Adler, A. "Implementing District-Wide Programs: If I Knew Then What I Know Now." The Fourth R, 57. 1995.

Amsler, T. "Educating for Citizenship: Reframing Conflict resolution Work in K-12 Schools." Paper presented at the Coulson Festshrift Meeting, Aspen Institute, Wye Conference Center, Queenstown, Maryland. March 13-14, 1994

Beekman, S., and J. Holmes. Battles, Hassles, Tantrums & Tears: Strategies for Coping with Conflict and Making Peace at Home. New York, NY: Hearst Books, William Morrow & Company, Inc., Publishers. 1993.

B. Benard. "Fostering Resiliency in Kids." Educational Leadership. Reprinted with permission of the Association for Supervision and Curriculum Development. (November) 1993.

Berger, Peter L., and Richard J. Neuhaus. "To Empower People: The Role of Mediation Structure in Public Policy, " Washington D.C.: American Enterprise Institute for Public Policy Research. 1977.

Bodeuhamer, Gregory. Parent In Control. U.S.A. 1995.

Bodine, R., and **R.D.** Crawford, and F. Schrumpt. Creating the Peaceable School: A

Comprehensive Program for Teaching Conflict Resolution. Champaign, IL: Research Press, Inc., 1994.

Carter, J. Talking Peace: A Vision for the Next Generation. New York, NY: Dutton Children's Books. 1993.

Catalano, R., and J.D. Hawkins. Communities That Care: Risk-Focused Prevention Using the Social Development Strategy. Seattle, WA: Developmental Research and Programs, Inc. 1995.

Copeland, N., and F. Garfield. Resolving Conflict: Activities for Grades K-3. Albuquerque, NM: Center for Dispute Resolutions. 1989.

Cox, J.D. Personal Communication. (May) 1996.

Crawford, D., R. Bodine, and R. Hoglund. The School for Quality Learning.

Champaign, IL: Research Press, Inc. 1993.

Cummings, Jeanne. Cox News Service, THE LUFKIN DAILY NEWS.

Goldberg, S.B., and H.J. Reske, "Talking with Attorney General Janet Reno," American Bar Association Journal, 1993.

Graham, Billy. "My Answers," CHICAGO TRIBUNE. New York: News Syndicate, Inc. (1960).

Graham, Billy. "Answers To Life's Problems," CHICAGO TRIBUNE. New York: News Syndicate, Inc. (1988).

Hamburg, D. Education for Conflict Resolution. Report of the President of the Carnegie Corporation of New York, 1994.

Harrington, Christine B. Shadow Justice: The Ideology and Institutionalization of Alternatives to Court, Boston: Little, Brown, and Company. 1985.

Holmberg, M., and J. Halligan. Conflict Management for Juvenile Treatment Facilities: A Manual for Training and Program Implementation. San Francisco, CA: Community Board Program, Inc. 1992.

Johnson, D.W., and R.T. Johnson. Teaching Students To Be Peacemakers. Edina, MN: Interaction Book Company. 1991.

Johnson, D., and R. Johnson. S"Cooperative Learning and Conflict Resolution." The Fourth R 42:8. 1993.

Laue, James. "The Conflict Resolution Movement: History, Problems, and Prospects" in Christian, T.F. (Ed.) Expanding Horizons: Theory and Research in Dispute Resolution-Dispute Resolution Papers Series No. 6. August 1989: Washington, D.C.: American Bar Association Standing Committee on Dispute Resolution. 1989.

Lowry, Randolph, and Richard W. Meyers. Conflict Management and Counseling. Volume 29 of the Resources for Christian Counseling Series. Copyright by Word, Inc. 1991.

McEwen, Craig A., and Richard J. Mainman. "Arbitration and Mediation as Alternatives to Court," Policies Studies Journal. 1982.

McEwen, Craig A. 1987. "Differing Visions of Alternative Dispute Resolution and Formal Law." The Justice System Journal. 12, 247-259.

Moore, P, and D. Batiste. "Preventing Youth Violence: Prejudice Elimination and Conflict Resolution Programs." Forum. No. 25 (Spring) 1994.

Harrington, Christine B. Shadow Justice: The Ideology and Institutionalization of Alternatives to Court. Westport: Greenwood Press, 1985.

In-Home Family Therapy, and Violence Tape. London: Larski Sand-Pringle, 1991j3. Konopka, G. "A Renewed Look at Human Development, Human Needs, and Human Services." Proceedings of the Annual Gisela Konopka Lectureship. St. Paul, MN: University of Minnesota Center for Youth Development and Research. 1985.

Kral, Ron., MS. Strategies That Work, Techniques For Solutions in School. 1995.

Lowry, L. Randolph; J.D. Richard and W. Meyers. Conflict Management and Counseling Vol. 29. United States of America, 1991.

PERC 101: Module 12. The Mediation. Arbitration, Negotiation Commandments. The Internet: http://www2.conflictresolution.org/perc/perc101/module12/mod12.html.

New American Standard Bible. Lockman Foundation, 1977.

New International Version, 1973, 1978, 1984, International Bible Society: Used by permission of Zondervon Bible Publishers.

NEW YORK TIMES NEWS SERVICE.

Prothrow-Stith, D. Violence Prevention: Curriculum for Adolescents. Newton, MA: Education Development Center. 1987.

Reno, J. "Attorney General Announces New Effort to Prevent School Violence." U.S. Department of Justice press release, May 29, 1996.

Sadalla, G.M., and M. Holmberg. Conflict Resolution: A Secondary Curriculum. San Francisco, CA: Community Board Program, Inc. 1987.

Sande, Ken. The Peacemaker. Printed in the United States of America (1991).

Sande, Ken. The Peacemaker. U.S.A.: Zondervan Bible Publisher. 1996.

Schmidt, F., and A. Friedman. Fighting Families. Miami, FL: Peace 10 Education Foundation. 1994.

Schrumpf, F., D. Crawford, and R. Bodine. Peer Mediation: Conflict Resolution in

Schools. Revised edition. Champaign, IL: Research Press, Inc. 1996. Sneve, V.D.H. "Women of the Circle." A Common Land, A Diverse People. H.

Thompson, A. Huseboe, and S. Looney (eds.). Sioux Falls, SD: Nordland Heritage Foundation, 1987.

Tape, 1991. In-Home Family Therapy and Violence. Aponte, Larski, Sand-Pringle, Lindon. AAMFT, Resource Leak.

The Holy Bible. I Corinthians 6:1 & 7.

The Lufkin Daily News, Sunday, August 17, 1997.

Vernon's Annotated Civil Practice & Remedies Volume 3, Chapter 154: St. Paul, Minn.: West Publishing Company. 1994.

Walter, John L., and James Peeler. Becoming Solution-focused in Brief Therapy. New York: 1992.

Washington Post, THE LUFKIN DAILY NEWS.

Yingling, Lynelle. "Basic Assumptions of Systems Family Therapy." East Texas State University.

York, Phyllis and David; and Ted Wachtel. Tough Love. New York: 1983.

author

D. YVONNE MARSHALL

Route 2, Box 248 • Huntington, Texas 75949 • Telephone (409) 422-5342

EDUCATION   Doctor of Philosophy and Psychology and Christian Counseling through Louisiana Baptist University Shreveport, Louisiana, May 1, 1998.

Marriage and Family Counselor, February 1998.

Certified Tobacco Addiction Counselor Clinical Practitioner, February 1998.

Social Work Associate Certification, 1984 - 1998

Certified Family Life Educator, 1991-1999

Master's of Science Degree from Nova University, Ft. Lauderdale, FL
- Major in Child/Youth Care, 1992

Master's Internship studies/ resource work on Drop-Out Preventions Program with on-site visits to classrooms and sitting in on curriculum taught

Bachelor's Degree from Stephen F. Austin State University, 1986
- Child Development & Social Work with related internship at Early Childhood Lab at Stephen F. Austin University and the welfare county courthouse

Project Head Start, 1979-1981 (195 Hours in Workshops)

EXPERIENCE

1996 - 1998   Deep East Texas Council of Government, Det/Try Star
**Family Based Services Specialist/Supervising Five Counties
and Five Counselors**
- Provide crisis intervention
- Individual, group and family counseling to effect behavior change
- Develop, review and monitor service plan
- Provide training to other case workers and family preservation theory and practice
- Prepare records and reports

1995 - 1996   Fantasy Photo
Marketing Director
- Book photo settings and sell prints in day cares, nursing homes, beauty shops, private homes, as well as in the studio
- Play Santa, Ms. Santa, the Easter Bunny-all special holidays with children
- School pictures, proms, plays, etc.

1993 - 1994   Buckner Family &Children Services
Program Specialist
- Family preservation-provided counseling and in-home services helping families discover ways to handle problems and keep children in the home
- Client assistance-helped families, individuals, and senior adults with
- medical needs; children with M/H and M/R disabilities, food, housing, job training, day care, legal assistance, and parenting skills
- Counseling services-available to meet a variety of needs, listen and offer guidance to individuals and families with problematic and abusive situations
- Adoption and maternity services-guidance to women facing unplanned pregnancies, assisted families interested in adoption
- Placement outreach service of foster care, as well as intake of information for other Buckner residential programs
- Worked with Adult probation and in related family crises

1993 - 1993   Hospice In The Pines
Social Worker
- Admitting Coordinator for intakes and referrals
- Admitting Social Worker-worked as a team with RN

1991 - 1993   Cornerstone M.H.M.R., 3213 So. Medford, Lufkin, TX
Contracted as Family Consultant
- Developed curriculum education on life skills, nutrition, child development, behavior management, and medical needs to parents referred by the Department of Human Services
- Conducted parents' meetings
- Counseled children and parents in family crises

1990 - 1991   Department of Human Services
Child Care Management Director
- Overall responsibility for all CCMS functions
- Supervised clerical, client service workers, and vendor management specialists
- Hired staff and wrote personnel policies, procedures
- Conducted meetings with current providers to explain new system, specific policies, and procedures
- Develop training plan for Department of Human Services approval

1988 - 1990   Cornerstone M.H.M.R.
Family Consultant
- Administered both home and center-based activities
- Planned and organized curriculum and ongoing developmental assessments, serving as a member of the intertransdisciplinary team
- Administered developmental programming for infants-birth to three years old
- Maintained all records according to procedure
- Advocate and case manager with outside agencies to coordinate services with chronically ill children and their parents
- Counseled with families dealing with death and grief after losing a child
- Served as team leader directing monthly meetings with other team members, working to strengthen and improve the quality of entire program
- Conducted parent meetings and training to parents and other staff
- Worked closely with other community agencies

1987 - 1988   Department of Human Services
Child Protective Specialist
- Planned and wrote service plans for parents
- Provided counseling, parenting, life skill, nutrition, child development, behavior management, medical needs, and guidance to individuals and families with problematic or abusive situations, working to keep children in the homes if possible
- On occasion had to place children in foster care or with another family member to get situation under control, making it safe for the child
- Conducted parent meetings, working closely with other community agencies, schools, doctors, judges, lawyers, and others in the community

1981 - 1986   Stephen F. Austin State University In-Home Educational Services
Educational Aide
- Developed and assisted curriculum education information on life skills, nutrition, child development, behavioral management, and medical needs to parents who have been referred to the program from the Department of Human Services
- Counseled with family crises in problematic families
- Internship in Early Childhood Lab at Stephen F. Austin University and welfare county courthouse in social work

1978 - 1981   Project Head Start
Home Visitor
- Provided basic education for preschool and assisted in provision of medical and dental services
- Conducted parent meetings, training to parents, working closely with other community agencies, schools, doctors, judges, lawyers and other professionals
- Provided health, hygiene, child development, and nutrition education
- to parents
- Conducted parent meetings with ocher community agencies
- Worked closely with doctors and teachers of community and with children with handicap disabilities

1971 - 1974   James R. Randal Orthopedic Elementary School, Clinton,
May 1974   Maryland Supervisor: Maureen Wakins
Substitute Teacher and Teacher's Aide
- Worked in Special Education classes and health room with *MIR* and M/H developmental disabilities
- Worked with OT and PTs and families

REFERENCES

Dean Stanley
School of Applied Arts and Sciences
Stephen F. Austin State University
(409) 468-4604

Dr. Barbara Flournoy Huntington,
TX 75949
(409) 422-5308

Winfred Adams, R.N.
State Department of Public Welfare
Home (409) 632-4251
Office (409) 632-7708

Betty J. Brown Workforce Director
Lufkin, Texas 75901
Office (409) 634-2247

Ellen P. Platt, Certified Public
Accountant
P.O. Box 393
Huntington, TX 75949
Home (409) 876-5697
Office (409) 637-3333
Angelina College
(409) 639-1301

Phyllis Burnett Administrative
Assistant Route 2
Huntington, Texas 75949
Home (409) 422-4924

www.ingramcontent.com/pod-product-compliance
Lightning Source LLC
Chambersburg PA
CBHW022059020426
42335CB00012B/750